Personal Wellness

Your Most Profitable Investment

Rick Griggs

A FIFTY-MINUTE™ SERIES BOOK

CRISP PUBLICATIONS, INC.
Menlo Park, California

PERSONAL WELLNESS
Your Most Profitable Investment

Rick Griggs

CREDITS
Editors: **Anne Knight and Tony Hicks**
Design and Composition: **Interface Studio**
Cover Design: **Carol Harris**
Artwork: **Ralph Mapson**

Copyright © 1990 by Crisp Publications, Inc.
Printed in the United States of America

English language Crisp books are distributed worldwide. Our major international distributors include:

CANADA: Reid Publishing Ltd., Box 69559—109 Thomas St., Oakville, Ontario, Canada L6J 7R4. TEL: (905) 842-4428, FAX: (905) 842-9327

Raincoast Books Distribution Ltd., 112 East 3rd Avenue, Vancouver, British Columbia, Canada V5T 1C8. TEL: (604) 873-6581, FAX: (604) 874-2711

AUSTRALIA: Career Builders, P.O. Box 1051, Springwood, Brisbane, Queensland, Australia 4127. TEL: 841-1061, FAX: 841-1580

NEW ZEALAND: Career Builders, P.O. Box 571, Manurewa, Auckland, New Zealand. TEL: 266-5276, FAX: 266-4152

JAPAN: Phoenix Associates Co., Mizuho Bldg. 2-12-2, Kami Osaki, Shinagawa-Ku, Tokyo 141, Japan. TEL: 3-443-7231, FAX: 3-443-7640

Selected Crisp titles are also available in other languages. Contact International Rights Manager Suzanne Kelly at (415) 323-6100 for more information.

Library of Congress Catalog Card Number 89-81519
Griggs, Rick
Personal Wellness
ISBN 1-56052-021-3

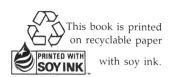

This book is printed on recyclable paper with soy ink.

TO THE READER

Healthy people live balanced lives. They maintain moderation in their habits and are excited about being alive. This book teaches the basics of healthy living and stresses that anyone wishing to can change his or her life in positive adventurous ways. Here's what you'll learn as you read this book:

BACK CARE—What healthy people do to avoid, correct, and/or minimize back problems. You don't have to become one of the millions whose backs give them trouble. You don't have to live with back pain.

EXERCISE—You don't need to become an exercise fanatic to reap the benefits of cardiovascular fitness and general good health. You will read about leisure activities and how they fit nicely into your plan for overall health.

NUTRITION—You've heard it before, but a quick review can't hurt. Did you know that the four food groups are on the four walls of your supermarket? This book offers nutrition tips for the 90s.

HEART HEALTH—Here you'll find useful information on what it takes to keep your heart healthy. There are a few things you cannot control, but many risk factors can be addressed to help you have a healthier heart.

CHOLESTEROL—The real scoop on this fatty stuff that can be good and bad. When it comes to cholesterol, there are HDLs and LDLs, and it's important to know the difference. Your total cholesterol count includes both, so a single measurement can be misleading.

SMOKING CONTROL—Practical ways to reduce or eliminate the smoking habit. There are no miracles, but behavioral psychology offers tested ways to enable anyone to adjust his or her living, eating, and working patterns so that smoking behavior can be changed and life expectancy lengthened.

WEIGHT CONTROL—Exactly why it's dangerous to lose too many pounds too fast. You'll read about how anyone can lose fat, gain muscle tone, lose inches, and still enjoy a fun and adventurous life.

STRESS MANAGEMENT—How to recognize and understand it. Some thrive on stress, others die, and still others just give up. Healthy people don't fear stress, but they don't let it control them. Make stress work for you, not against you.

(continued next page)

TO THE READER (Continued)

ALCOHOL AND DRUGS—Most people don't abuse alcohol or drugs. Many, however, do and suffer from the disease of substance abuse. Learn how to recognize warning signs and avoid the serious health problems that result from misused alcohol and drugs.

HOW TO RELAX—You've been trained to get up on time, get to school or work on time, and accomplish great things. Aren't you supposed to enjoy the journey? Kids can't wait to grow up, students can't wait to graduate, and workers count the days to retirement. Why not enjoy life along the way? Healthy people learn to put work and worries aside and relax. Read about some daredevil ideas for changing your habits so you can learn to relax.

HELPING FAMILY AND OTHERS—If you've ever tried to change the behavior of someone else, you know it's not easy. Maybe it's none of your business. Try to personally achieve some of the 11 changes in this section before attempting to influence someone else. Have fun!

SEXUAL DISEASES, AIDS, AND CANCER—As we enter the 90s, one of the hottest topics is the change in sexual attitudes. Much of this results from the epidemic problem of sexually transmitted diseases (STDs). Syphilis and gonorrhea are still with us but have been joined by herpes and AIDS (Acquired Immune Deficiency Syndrome). The healthy person should know the facts and take precautions. Do you know the seven warning signs for cancer?

A BALANCED LIFE—Read about **macro** and **micro** balance. Here are some useful ideas for keeping your life in order. The major segments of your life should be balanced in relation to other major segments. Each segment also needs to have internal balance.

WELLNESS AFFIRMATIONS—These are short statements that help you internalize the parts of this book you want to remember. By repeating the affirmations, your subconscious mind will help guide you toward your goals.

GREAT EXCUSES—There are some whoppers at the end of the book—excuses that people make for not improving their wellness. If friends or family use these, you'll be prepared to say ''I've heard that one ... let's go.''

Enjoy the book and ''here's to good health''!

Rick Griggs

CONTENTS

DEDICATION

To my mother Suzanne Sutton, who studied, taught, and lived health and wellness principles decades before they became popular in advertising and in university research labs. Her challenge was to convince her children not only to believe in healthy living but also to practice it. We haven't forgotten!

ACKNOWLEDGMENTS

When I think of getting through high school and college with a healthy mind and body, two people come to mind. Thank you coaches Ed Taylor and Aubrey Chevalier. And I'll always be thankful for the useful information from Marilynn Tobias and the help and patience of Lorraine Pursell, Sherian Schroder, and Mary Diggins. I'm also grateful for the fast action when I needed it from Bob Cuenca, Mike Elsesser, and Marc Evans.

INTRODUCTION TO WELLNESS

Wellness is more than the absence of disease. It involves personal responsibility for one's own health. Wellness means taking positive steps to avoid disease and injury and live a lifestyle that promotes health, vigor, and energy.

By examining a continuum of wellness attitudes we can see that disease and wellness are poles apart.

DISEASE	**ABSENCE OF DISEASE**	**WELLNESS**
usually sick debilitating expensive life threatening	occasionally sick often tired mentally dragging ok attitude	rarely sick plenty of energy enjoyment of life great attitude

People's attitudes toward their personal health may differ widely. See where your attitudes and opinions fit in. Your goal should be to end up in the balanced box.

THREE ATTITUDES TO HEALTH

1.   NEGATIVE
You can't avoid sickness.
Doctors just get rich.
We'll all die anyway.

2.   DON'T CARE
Don't go to doctors.
Don't plan activities.
Neutral about wellness.

3.   BALANCED
Moderation is good.
Everyone controls their health.
Plan to live a long life.
Bright future (a few rough spots).

Wellness Affirmation

GENERAL HEALTH: Overall, I'm healthy and plan to remain so. My lifestyle is in a good healthy balance. I believe in consistency, moderation, and variety. I don't go overboard in any area because I want to enjoy life. This I affirm.

ED'S STORY

A SUCCESS STORY
"GREAT RESULTS FROM SMALL CHANGES"

It really is possible to change your lifestyle. Here's Ed's story in his own words, about how a series of small changes improved his health and general well-being.

Here is my perspective on the importance of achieving and maintaining a state of good health. I am now 48 years old, and until about a year or two ago, I never placed much importance on being physically fit. I had always been skeptical of lectures from medical doctors and others on the subjects of nutrition and exercise and their effect on your state of health. And when it came to exercise, I thought the normal physical demands of living (such as walking to the car, mowing the lawn, etc.) would suffice. My confrontation with reality came when my personal physician reviewed with me the results of an annual physical checkup. He said my cholesterol was 231 and my blood pressure and pulse rate were also slightly above normal. I said, "Why should I be concerned about that?" He said that the results of my physical exam, when used to calculate the cardiovascular risk factor index, show that I had a 20 percent greater than normal chance of experiencing a cardiovascular problem (heart attack, stroke, etc.).

Since I am an engineer by training and a quality manager by profession, he got my immediate attention. I understand cause and effect relationships and have a strong belief in probability statistics as a predictor of future results. So I said, "What do you want me to do, because I will not be satisfied until I am at or below average risk?" The doctor told me to:

- *Exercise at least three times a week for a minimum of 20 minutes at my cardiovascular conditioning target pulse rate.*

- *Take 2 grams a day of niacinimide as a cholesterol reducer.*

- *Take one aspirin a day as a blood clot preventative.*

- *Come back every three months for a re-evaluation of my condition (with blood tests) until the life-style changes had corrected the situation.*

(continued next page)

A SUCCESS STORY (continued)

I went away feeling a bit depressed. The thought of steak, ice cream, eggs, and bacon flashed through my mind. Oh well, I had better at least try, for I am not one who admits defeat easily. I started to think of some positive motivators. The thought of living long enough and being in good health to enjoy grandchildren and a life of ease after retirement replaced the thoughts of what I would be missing. I started eating chicken, fish, vegetables, fruits, oat and wheat bran muffins, and found that they were as good as the things I had given up (maybe not quite as good as cheesecake or a banana split, but close enough). I found restaurants in the area that serve a delicious variety of low-cholesterol foods. For exercise, I started on a combination of stationary bike at home for bad weather, and either brisk walking (4 miles in 1 hour at lunch), hiking or moderate mountain climbing (no sheer walls for me!) on occasion.

Well, did it work? I visited my doctor recently and received the following report:

- *Cholesterol down to 162.*

- *Blood pressure below average at 104/68.*

- *Pulse rate normal.*

- *Risk factor 66 percent less than average.*

My doctor said, ''If most people would listen to me like you did, I would have to find another line of work. People wouldn't need me to cure their ills.'' It is rewarding to be able to change those things that can be changed. I plan to continue through life with my new lifestyle and enjoy life more than ever.

Ed's story shows that it is possible for busy people to take care of their health and all the pressing issues of life. You'll see many Wellness Affirmations in this book. Use them to imprint positive wellness ideas into your brain. Find the ones most useful to you, and repeat them each day.

PART I

YOUR WELLNESS FOUNDATION

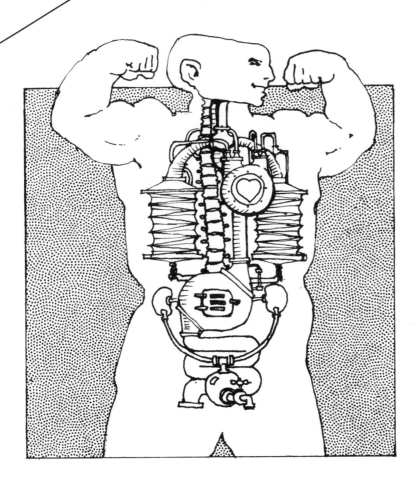

BACK CARE

Back pain is the number one complaint of people visiting doctors. On any given day in the United States, 6.5 million people are in bed with back problems. Four out of five people can expect back problems at some time in their lives. Unless you've been one of the unlucky victims, it's hard to believe that one physical ailment can cause so much pain, disruption, and frustration.

Some medical experts believe that people create 90 percent of their back problems. That sounds exaggerated, but even if the number is 70 percent, or only 40 percent, this is reason enough to study the causes of back pain and how to avoid problems.

The Pain: Back problems can be either acute or chronic. Causes of acute back pain include mechanical strain and overuse. Chronic problems usually stem from deteriorating vertebrae, discs, or other parts of the spine. Both acute and chronic pain are often linked to lack of muscle conditioning.

Causes: Back pain can be caused by injury, disease, or even psychological factors. If the pain persists, it is important to get the advice of a competent professional before continuing regular activities. Whether the pain started because of heredity, your job, hobbies, sports activities, childhood injuries, posture, diet, nutrition, pregnancy, sedentary lifestyles, or bad treatment the main thing is to find a way to correct the pain.

What Can You Do? People try everything to fix bad backs. They dabble with yoga, traction, rolfing, and shiatsu. They try electric stimulation, drugs, gravity inversion, and even neurosurgery. What have you tried? Write your answers in the spaces below.

What has caused back pain for me in the past?

_____

_____

What helped reduce my back pain?

_____

_____

What didn't help?

_____

_____

| "Health is not a condition of matter, but of mind" | —Mary Baker Eddy |

DO THIS TO REDUCE BACK PAIN

Now that we've discussed the background for back pain and you've listed some personal causes and solutions. Let's look at what health care professionals suggest, (assuming the back is not injured to the point of requiring surgery).

Hot and Cold: Try a warm bath, a hot water bottle, or 15-minute intervals of heat followed by cold. Don't burn or freeze your back in the process. Try warm and cool just to be safe. Many people try wearing thermal underwear to retain heat. Heat increases the flexibility and circulation in and around muscles, tendons, ligaments, and joints. The cold eases the pain and reduces swelling.

Weight Control: You do wonders for your back when you remove extra body fat and replace it with good, solid muscle. This substitution of muscle for fat will help reduce back problems. Excess weight adds to the load your back must handle.

Massage: Rhythmical pressure application relaxes muscles and dissipates pain. It's more useful for acute strains rather than for chronic problems.

Exercises: Exercise in general, helps to stretch both the joints in the spine and improve muscle strength so that less is required of the bones and joints in the spine. Strong abdominal muscles are excellent weapons against back pain. A word of caution: Never exercise when you have severe pain or back spasms.

Manipulation: Manipulation of the back and spine by competent professionals such as a chiropractor can be beneficial for mechanical problems such as spinal lesions and derangements (dislocations, subluxed joint, or loss of mobility). Manipulation cannot repair a burst disc or a damaged ligament.

Supports: Sometimes an artificial back support provides short-term relief or allows healing and reduction of inflammation. Options include spinal corsets and plaster casts. A heat-moldable section can be warmed and then molded to an individual patient's back. This limits back movement and decreases the pressure load on the back. The disadvantage of this support is that if it's worn too long, vital muscles may become weakened.

How About Water? Some health and wellness practitioners believe that deep-water exercises offer great benefits for those with back problems. Water offers the following benefits:

- Noncompressive environment (non–weight bearing)
- Water buoyancy—floating
- Hydrostatic pressure—water pressing consistently against the body

These benefits are valuable in therapy because they allow more range of motion and better support, while reducing pain. (Source: Mike Elsesser, Marc Evans.)

WHAT I CAN DO TO AVOID BACK PAIN?

Look at the list below. Put a check mark next to the things you're already doing. Then check those things you decide to incorporate in your regular routine.

BACK PAIN AVOIDANCE	I'm doing this	I intend to start doing this
Maintain an open, positive attitude.	☐	☐
Lift heavy objects by bending at the knees (*not* bending my back).	☐	☐
Support my back while sleeping (firm mattress, sleep on side with knees bent).	☐	☐
Support my back while sitting (both feet on floor, knees higher than hips).	☐	☐
Correct posture (stand tall, chin in, pelvis forward, buttocks in).	☐	☐
Take warm tub baths.	☐	☐
Apply moist heat while in bed.	☐	☐
Use cold to reduce spasms.	☐	☐
Use self-massage.	☐	☐
Exercise consistently.	☐	☐
Take regular ''back breaks.''	☐	☐
Walk 2 miles each day.	☐	☐
Carry objects comfortably.	☐	☐
Avoid surgery.	☐	☐
Learn about medications before using them.	☐	☐
Wear good shoes.	☐	☐
Join a health club and work out regularly.	☐	☐
Swim weekly.	☐	☐
Move the car seat forward.	☐	☐
Keep both hands on the steering wheel.	☐	☐
Eat properly.	☐	☐
Lose weight if indicated.	☐	☐
Wear a back support when necessary.	☐	☐
Hang from a chinning bar.	☐	☐
Follow my physician's or chiropractor's advice.	☐	☐

Wellness Affirmation

BACK CARE: I control the health of my back. I do what is needed and see a physician when called for. Back care includes balance in exercise, eating, and relaxation. I will keep doing the things that build a healthy back and minimize pain.

EXERCISE AND WELLNESS

Think of your body as an automobile engine. To work most efficiently, it needs to be driven carefully and properly maintained. It is not good for your car to sit unused for long periods of time. Likewise, it is damaging to race it to the limit. The best approach is to drive it regularly—allowing it to warm up before driving it hard.

Like an automobile engine, when you screech out of the driveway with an exercise program, you risk tearing your engine apart, damaging your frame, and/or fouling up your cooling system.

FORMULA FOR FITNESS

The exercise formula for good cardiorespiratory fitness is to exercise for 15–30 minutes three times a week, with your heart rate in the target zone. In other words, to stay fit you should get a good workout about every other day.

The TARGET ZONE is where your heart rate should be while exercising to get fit but not to get sick. *Rule of thumb:* If you can carry on a light conversation, and breathe easily, without sweating heavily, you are probably in your target zone. Use the calculations below to find the upper and lower limits of your target zone.

1. MAXIMUM HEART RATE = 220 minus your age.

   For a 30-year-old: 220 minus 30 = 190.
   For a 55-year-old: 220 minus 55 = 165.
   For you: 220 minus _____ = _____.

2. UPPER LIMIT OF TARGET ZONE = Maximum heart rate multiplied by .80

   For a 30-year-old: 190 × .80 = 152.
   For a 55-year-old: 165 × .80 = 132.
   For you: _____ × .80 = _____.

3. LOWER LIMIT OF TARGET ZONE = Maximum heart rate multiplied by .60

   For a 30-year-old: 190 × .60 = 114.
   For a 55-year-old: 165 × .60 = 99.
   For you: _____ × .60 = _____.

WHAT IS A GOOD WORKOUT?

*Penny is 40 years old and wants to begin working out. She wants to keep her weight down and stay young and healthy looking. She likes to jog fast but remembers about exercising in her **target zone** (page 10) for health improvement and safety. At 40 she figures her **maximum heart rate** should be 220 − 40 = 180. She also knows that while she's jogging she should keep her pulse (beats per minute) between 60 and 80 percent of this number. Using the chart on page 13, she finds that her pulse should be between 108 and 144 beats per minute. This is Penny's ideal training zone.*

*Roberto is a show-off. At 37, he's still good at sports and he likes others to know it. He was thoroughly engrossed in playing a tough game of soccer one Saturday afternoon, when suddenly he became dizzy and light-headed. He noticed that his heart was pounding wildly. His friend Alex took a quick exercise pulse and found that Roberto's heart rate was 166. Some quick figuring (220 − 37 = 183) revealed that the show-off was close to his maximum heart rate. In fact, he was 20 heart beats a minute **over** the top of his training zone. The danger, for Roberto, is that he could have had a heart attack while pushing his cardiovascular system past its limit.*

"The golden rule is moderation in all things."	—Terence

EXERCISE: LOVE IT OR HATE IT

A good first step is to decide what you would enjoy and what you know you would hate. Even if your passions aren't extreme, you may find preferences in either direction. You're more likely to engage in the kind of exercise that you enjoy, so set yourself up for success by selecting wisely.

In the list below, check the exercises you enjoy. Cross out those you hate. Put a question mark next to the ones you're not sure about.

EXERCISES I LOVE

☐ jogging ☐ handball ☐ soccer
☐ running ☐ tennis ☐ football
☐ bicycling ☐ hockey ☐ racquetball
☐ swimming ☐ weightlifting ☐ badminton
☐ baseball ☐ aerobics ☐ lacrosse
☐ volleyball ☐ gymnastics ☐ walking

EXERCISES I HATE

☐ jogging ☐ handball ☐ soccer
☐ running ☐ tennis ☐ football
☐ bicycling ☐ hockey ☐ racquetball
☐ swimming ☐ weightlifting ☐ badminton
☐ baseball ☐ aerobics ☐ lacrosse
☐ volleyball ☐ gymnastics ☐ walking

Add any that come to mind that aren't listed.

> **CAUTION:** Every year, hundreds of people die from sudden heart failure while exercising or overexerting themselves. This means that they were **above the top end** of their target or training zone. A physical activity (such as shoveling snow, running a race or playing tennis) can be performed safely while you are in good shape. It, however, can be deadly if you have not been physically active. In the United States *every single minute* someone suffers a heart attack. Other industralized nations are not much different. As you will read in the section on Heart Health, information, precautions, and early response are vital. One-half of all first heart attacks end in death. As a moderate exerciser, you should become familiar with the heart rate charts shown on the facing page.

TARGET HEART RATE CHARTS

FULL-MINUTE PULSE

Take your pulse while you exercise. Many bicyclists and other athletes have found safe methods for taking their pulse for a full minute while continuing to exercise. They know that as soon as they stop, their pulse will begin to slow down.

Age	Maximum Pulse Rate	Lower Limit (60% of Maximum)	Upper Limit (80% of Maximum)
75	145	87	116
70	150	90	120
65	155	93	124
60	160	96	128
55	165	99	132
50	170	102	136
45	175	105	140
40	180	108	144
35	185	111	148
30	190	114	152
25	195	117	156
20	200	120	160

6-SECOND EXERCISE PULSE

This pulse should be taken as soon as you stop exercising. To avoid getting dizzy and overtaxing your heart, slow down but don't stop completely. The first six seconds after you slow down is usually an accurate time to measure what your heart was doing while you were exercising.

Age	Maximum Pulse Rate	Lower Limit (60% of Maximum)	Upper Limit (80% of Maximum)
75	14	8	12
70	15	9	12
65	15	9	12
60	16	9	13
55	16	10	13
50	17	10	13
45	17	10	14
40	18	11	14
35	18	11	15
30	19	11	15
25	19	12	15
20	20	12	16

A short cut: Take your six-second pulse and add a zero (0) to get the full-minute count. When using the six-second pulse, try to count half-beats because they represent a full five beats on the full-minute chart.

EXERCISE AND WELLNESS (Continued)

FIVE FITNESS AREAS

If your goal is to be physically fit, you should consider five areas when deciding what activities to pursue. Those who understand a broad wellness philosophy maintain a balanced attitude toward physical fitness. The five areas are:

MUSCLE STRENGTH—the force of a single muscle contraction.

MUSCLE ENDURANCE—the repeated action of a group of muscles over time.

CARDIOVASCULAR EFFICIENCY—the efficient exchange of oxygen for waste gases and other products (also known as circulorespiratory efficiency).

BODY FAT—the percentage of total body fat in relation to lean body mass.

FLEXIBILITY—the range of motion in the tendons, ligaments, muscles, and joints.

That's a lot to worry about! What do you do to include all of these five areas into a well-rounded program and still take care of daily responsibilities? This is a challenge. Let's see how Carol, a single mother did it:

Carol, a single mother is determined to take good care of her 8-year-old son and keep herself healthy. It takes about 40 minutes to get him ready for school. On her way home, she swings by her gym for an early morning aerobics class. This eliminates a second trip, and because she's made several friends in the class, there is built-in motivation to attend, even when she feels like skipping. She varies her workout routine to make sure it includes stretching and light work with the weights. She covers all five fitness components. Carol says that by taking care of herself, she's better able to provide care for her son.

Wellness Affirmation

EXERCISE: I am a consistent and moderate exerciser. I've adjusted my life to include many types of activity. I'm stronger, more alert, and much better off. It's part of my life.

LEISURE ACTIVITIES

Studies prove that engaging in consistent and moderate activity helps keep you healthy. The good news is that you don't have to beat your brains out in the pool or in the gym to stay well and healthy. Your mind has plenty to do with wellness. Whenever you get involved in less-strenuous activities that you enjoy, you are improving your wellness.

These less-strenuous leisure activities may not improve cardiovascular fitness, but they correlate well with being healthy, happy, and relaxed.

Leisure activities are at the lower end of the fitness scale only in terms of intensity and direct benefit to the body's cardiovascular and respiratory systems. The less strenuous type of activity is ideally suited for changing one's lifestyle. Here are some of the reasons.

Leisure activities are beneficial because:
- Most are safe.
- Few result in sudden death due to overexertion.
- Many combine socializing with exercising.
- Competition is usually minimal.
- It's easier to build a lifelong habit with them.

HUMMING ALONG AT A SLOWER PACE

You may be thinking about exciting and exhilarating activities you do in your leisure time. They certainly aren't slowpoke activities! The point is that while some activities physically strengthen your body, others do great things to relax your mind and body. Both are valuable and essential.

Enid and Brian aren't into heavy exercises. They're getting older and Brian's back occasionally gives him trouble. Enid tried aggressive aerobics classes at the height of the fitness boom and kept injuring herself. Both Enid and Brian are convinced that their slower pace (golf, striding, and weekly birdwatching trips) keep them healthy and happy, without the injuries.

This couple is doing fine. As they continue with their generally active lifestyle, they are receiving the health and wellness benefits they need. If their exercise is regular (3–4 times a week), and includes fast walking and some hills, their health will be even better.

Leisure Activities (continued)

You don't have to go overboard on anything to be healthy. When you participate in activities you enjoy, you are doing things to balance your life.

From the list below, check the activities you enjoy. Cross out ones you don't enjoy. Put a question mark next to the ones you're not sure about.

ACTIVITIES I ENJOY

☐ bowling   ☐ driving range   ☐ walking
☐ lawn bowling   ☐ birdwatching   ☐ astronomy
☐ miniature golf   ☐ golfing   ☐ cricket
☐ fishing   ☐ hiking   ☐ boating

ACTIVITIES I DON'T ENJOY

☐ bowling   ☐ driving range   ☐ walking
☐ lawn bowling   ☐ birdwatching   ☐ astronomy
☐ miniature golf   ☐ golf course   ☐ cricket
☐ fishing   ☐ hiking   ☐ boating

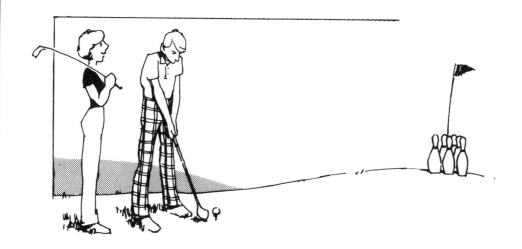

LET'S COMBINE ACTIVITIES

THIRTEEN EXERCISE DO'S

It's confusing out there! Much that you read and hear about exercising sometimes seems contradictory. Following, however, is an excellent foundation for a good general exercise plan.

1. Have fun with whatever you do.

2. Do some activity every day so that exercise becomes a daily habit.

3. Do engage in moderate to vigorous activity three times a week for fitness conditioning (or cardiovascular fitness).

4. Do get a medical check-up before starting an exercise program, especially if you're over 35, have a history of illness, or have become a couch potato.

5. Do learn to take your pulse in beats-per-minute while resting and exercising.

6. Do develop friends with whom to share your physical activities.

7. Do say ''yes'' when you're asked to participate in games, workouts, walks, or other types of social exercise.

8. Do make your exercise sessions last 20–40 minutes.

9. Do reward yourself mentally.

10. Do reward yourself with something tangible as well, such as a new pair of athletic shoes.

11. Do cultivate a positive mental attitude about your healthy body until it becomes natural.

12. Do set goals for health and fitness improvement and revise them every few weeks.

13. Do remember, if you can't complete a full workout, at least do something. For instance, go for a walk, ride a bike for 5 minutes, or swing the racket or club a few times just to build the habit.

SEVEN EXERCISE DON'TS

We try to avoid negatives. But with exercise as with most other life activities, there are a few things to eliminate or avoid. Take a look at the following list of ''Don'ts'' to see where you might change to improve your personal wellness.

1. Don't make major, abrupt changes in your activity level. Your body hates surprises. Work slowly and gradually to build up to your goals.

2. Don't try to keep up with a friend or partner who's been performing an activity longer than you. Remember, you're building lifelong habits, not trying to win a short race.

3. Don't discount your body's signs of distress (heavy sweating or breathing, chest pains, dizziness, frequent accidents, or injuries).

4. Don't lose momentum. It's harder to start over than it is to keep on with your routine.

5. Don't get into a rut. Overdoing the same sport or exercise can lead to boredom, injuries, and feelings of dread (''Do I have to do it again today?'').

6. Don't become fanatical. Stay balanced. Be consistent, be moderate, and add variety to your exercise routine.

7. Don't become injured or ill as a result of your program. Know when to go easy or even change your usual pattern of exercising.

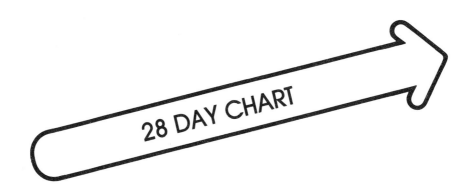

28 DAY CHART

28-DAY EXERCISE CHART

"IF YOU CAN DO IT FOR 28 DAYS...YOU CAN DO IT FOREVER"

Your 28-day exercise chart is a tool to make your progress visible and rewarding. Use it as a positive tool for ongoing improvement in your life. When it becomes a chore, or a source of guilt, toss it. By that time it has lost its usefulness.

Start today (or tomorrow, if it's already late as you read this). Begin with an easy, achievable goal. To be consistent, fill out the chart at the same time each day. You'll notice that this chart, and others like it throughout the book, only have 28 days each. We'll talk about the missing days later.

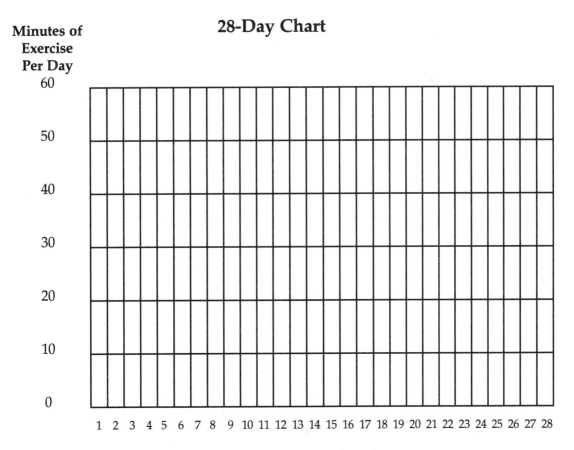

WHAT ABOUT THE MISSING DAYS? Read on!

THE COST OF LAZINESS

"COUCH POTATOES COST A LOT"

WHAT IS A COUCH POTATO? Just because you watch a little TV (6 hours a day), eat a few chips (2 bags), and sip on a couple soft drinks (a six-pack), does that mean you're a bona fide couch potato? Well, so what if you do the above, it doesn't cost a lot of money, right? Wrong!

HOW MUCH DO COUCH POTATOES COST EMPLOYERS? What do you think? Check the answer you think is right and compare your answer with the box at the bottom of the page.

☐ $1,900 a year
☐ $1,200 a year
☐ $810 a year
☐ $425 a year
☐ $150 a year

Above costs include:
- Less work (therefore less taxes paid)
- Medical services
- Insurance benefits
- Disability payments

Answer: $1,900 a year (according to *Longevity* magazine).

NUTRITION AND WELLNESS

Consider for a moment that your body is like a cherished car that you plan never to sell. As your dream machine ages, you will notice subtle changes in both appearance and performance.

You have a choice as to how you respond to these changes. You can choose to:

A. Trash the car, with no concern for the future.
B. Sell it to another person.
C. Hide its defects, instead of correcting them.
D. Provide on-going care in order to maintain the machine in top condition.

When the "car" is your body, the option to sell it and get a new one doesn't exist. Your body is yours until your final day. How you maintain it is up to you. Following are some nutrition basics that can make your machine hum!

THIRTEEN NUTRITION DO'S

1. Do eat 2–3 balanced meals each day.

2. Do shop from the four basic food groups. These are:
   1. grains and cereals   2. fruits and vegetables   3. meat and protein and 4. dairy products

3. Do include a variety of foods at each meal. Look for different colors, different textures, and even the amount of chewing each requires.

4. Do eat fish 2–3 times each week, choosing a variety of kinds.

5. Do eat slowly enough for your body to register that you've had enough.

6. Do eat with someone at least once a day. Socializing tends to reduce overeating, which is often based on negative emotions and feelings.

7. Do drink 5–8 glasses of water a day, preferably when your stomach is nearly empty.

8. Do pamper yourself and splurge once in a while. Life is good, and enjoyment in eating should be a source of pleasure. All the do's and don'ts still allow for some fun.

9. Do use polyunsaturated fats. These are liquid at room temperature.

10. Do learn the cholesterol levels of foods, and keep your cholesterol intake low.

11. Do remember that what you eat affects your performance. Examples include test-taking, sporting events, making speeches, and writing reports.

12. Do spread out food intake throughout the day. Studies show that this improves digestion and increases your metabolism (energy burning).

13. Do eat in a comfortable and pleasant atmosphere to tie eating in with your healthy and enjoyable lifestyle.

YOU SHOULD EAT LIKE ... A CAVEMAN???

You don't believe it? Well, there just may be some value in eating like a caveman.

How about stopping by after work for some peanut shells? *Sounds a bit strange, but this could make all of us live a lot longer says Professor Vaughn Bryant, Jr. from Texas A&M University. He thinks that the prehistoric caveman's diet of uncooked plants acted like a ''cleansing pad'' going through the intestines. It may not sound appealing but doctors say, strange as it may seem, this helps with several types of cancer.*

Professor Bryant believes that the extra roughage does wonders for weight control. Your stomach doesn't know the difference between ''pizza and peanut shells.''

Eating peanut shells may be going a bit far, but adding roughage to your diet in the form of fruits and vegetables is a great idea for keeping your digestive system clean and reducing the risk of colon cancer.

WHAT ABOUT FISH?

Amid all the commercials, ads, and billboards telling you what to do, here's an area where you can trust the benefits to be as good as the claims. Eating fish is one of the healthiest things you can do. It has direct effect in helping to reduce coronary heart disease by lowering blood cholesterol.

Forget the pills. Eat fresh fish. Don't plan on any miracles to immediately unclog arteries, lose 50 pounds, or become amazingly attractive. Eating fish is simply a healthy diet that reduces the risk of heart disease. The benefits of eating fish include:

1. Low in overall fat.
2. Low in saturated fat and calories.
3. High in Omega 3 fatty acids (great for the body). (It's more beneficial that you get these Omega 3 fatty acids from fish rather than capsules. Supplements have not shown the same benefits.)
4. Less room in the diet for red meat.

Remember, fish is great for reducing weight, dropping inches, and lowering the bad type of cholesterol. Cultures where fish is a main part of the diet show fewer signs of heart disease and have less trouble with obesity.

SEVEN NUTRITION DON'TS

1. Don't diet. Never. Erase the word diet from your vocabulary. Dieting causes more physical and psychological harm than you can imagine. Dieting is linked to weight *gain*, heart attacks, chemical imbalances, and substance abuse.

2. Don't skip meals. Eat regularly, especially in the morning. This insures a steady fuel supply to your brain and body while minimizing the effects of occasional coffee, alcohol, and sugar consumption.

3. Don't make the meal a secondary activity. Devote yourself fully to eating and enjoying the experience to its fullest. Don't eat while watching television, driving, telephoning, or cleaning.

4. Don't eat standing up or from refrigerator containers. Eating should be relaxed and comfortable. Eating is not an isolated event, but a component of your entire lifestyle.

5. Don't overuse alcohol, especially without eating. Alcohol is high in calories and overconsumption supresses the appetite. It is, of course, deadly on the road.

6. Don't eat late in the evening. Give your body time to digest your evening meal and wind down for a restful sleep. Some researchers argue that more fat is stored from late meals than from early ones.

7. Don't make a habit of eating at odd hours. Healthy bodies thrive on consistency, and react negatively to abrupt and irregular changes.

TODAY'S SPECIAL IS BACON WITH OUR FAMOUS BUTTER CREAM SAUCE!

THE HORRORS OF DIETING

Diet books are best sellers because the same people keep buying them. A dieter tries a new fad after every holiday and before every swimsuit season. There are better ways to control your weight than going on crash diets or fad programs.

Following are two cases where dieting was involved. See if you recognize yourself or someone else in these cases of chronic dieters.

1. *Frances was looking forward to the holidays. It would be fun to see Mom and Dad and attend parties with old friends. The only problem was her weight. She had ballooned 50 pounds above her high school weight. She visited a bookstore and purchased a book about a new diet that movie stars were using. The book promised that Frances would never be hungry and would shed 30 pounds in two weeks. Four weeks later Frances had lost 20 pounds, but she was sick in bed. She recovered to make the trip home, but regained the 20 pounds plus an extra seven pounds by February of the new year.*

2. *Jennifer read seven or eight diet books and tried some pretty weird stuff to lose weight. Three months ago, she heard a registered dietitian speak on weight control. Jennifer threw away her diet books along with all her special powders and liquids. She began eating three small meals each day. She actually loaded up on fruits and vegetables and different types of fish. She started drinking five glasses of water a day. At first, she was disappointed because results were not fast. But soon, she realized that she was losing 2–3 pounds a week. It didn't seem like much at first, but she remembered what the dietitian said about slow weight loss being much better than dropping pounds quickly. Something about building good habits for a lifetime, without suffering unnecessarily. In three months, Jennifer felt great and had dropped 24 pounds.*

Whatever you do, try to include a variety of foods in your diet. One study says that daily intake of potassium can reduce the risk of stroke. A stroke is like a heart attack in your brain. It kills tissue by cutting off the blood supply. If you include a daily serving of fruit or vegetables (potatoes, bananas, oranges, dates, avocados, apricots) and even fish (sardines and flounder) researchers claim you'll cut your risk of stroke. You won't need to worry about every new study that is published if you naturally include moderate amounts of many different foods in your diet.

GRAZING, LIKE THE COWS
BUT DON'T EAT THEM

Here's an idea that doesn't conform to the normal recommendations about eating and nutrition. Keep in mind that many current recommendations were once thought to be extreme and even dangerous. See what you think about the cows.

Have you ever lived on a farm or visited one? If you have, you probably noticed that cows do the same thing all day long....Right—they eat or graze throughout the day. For humans, the idea of "grazing" is to eat several small meals or snacks a day instead of larger, regular meals. The thinking is that if healthy food is spread out more evenly and consistently the body can metabolize it better, and you end up storing less fat. Your body's internal regulator, or metabolism, isn't worried about starving—so there's no need to store fat to ward off that danger. Some say that energy levels increase and digestion is improved.

Some university studies have discovered that spreading food intake, by eating several smaller meals, actually lowers LDL cholesterol. This works by keeping insulin levels in the body at a steady state. The pancreas does not need to react to a large load of food by releasing extra insulin (which makes the liver produce more cholesterol).

A warning however, grazing does not mean eating junk food, or constantly eating. It simply means healthy snacks are spaced throughout the day. Your total intake should not increase—only the number of times you stop what you are doing in order to eat.

Wellness Affirmation

NUTRITION: I eat well. I understand and apply the basic principles of nutrition. The effects on my body and mind are positive and clear. Eating well adds many benefits to my life. I plan to continue a sound nutritional program.

MY EATING INVENTORY*

SHOPPING: Start by buying groceries from all four food groups. List some of your favorites in each category. Use the list when you shop.

1. GRAINS and CEREALS
_____
_____
_____

2. MEAT, BEANS, and OTHER PROTEINS
_____
_____
_____

3. DAIRY PRODUCTS
_____
_____
_____

4. FRUITS and VEGETABLES
_____
_____
_____

REGULAR MEALS: Check the food groups you include at each meal.

BREAKFAST	LUNCH	DINNER
☐ Grains and cereals	☐ Grains and cereals	☐ Grains and cereals
☐ Meat, beans and other proteins	☐ Meat, beans and other proteins	☐ Meat, beans and other proteins
☐ Dairy products	☐ Dairy products	☐ Dairy products
☐ Fruits and vegetables	☐ Fruits and vegetables	☐ Fruits and vegetables

SNACKING: List the foods you snack on most.

_____   _____
_____   _____
_____   _____

SKIPPED MEALS: Which meals do you skip? Why?

☐ Breakfast (because _____)
☐ Lunch (because _____)
☐ Dinner (because _____)

Assess your eating inventory to see if there are major areas you want to change. Perhaps you're missing a basic food group, or snacking on too many salty foods. Are you consistently skipping a meal? Try to make small improvements, too. They can last your lifetime.

---

* Reprinted from *Professional Balance* by Rick Griggs. To order a copy write Crisp Publications, Inc., 95 First Street, Los Altos, CA 94022.

28-DAY NUTRITION CHART

"IF YOU CAN DO IT FOR 28 DAYS... YOU CAN DO IT FOREVER"

Here's a nutrition 28-day chart. You can use it as a tool to make your progress visible and rewarding. If this type of recording becomes a chore, or a source of guilt, toss it—by that time it has lost its usefulness. It should be used as a positive tool for ongoing improvement in your life.

Start either today or tomorrow. Begin with an easy, achievable goal. To be consistent, fill out the chart at the same time each day. Use the letter *W* for a glass of water and a *B, L,* or *D* to signify breakfast, lunch or dinner.

A wonderful goal might be to eat three meals and drink five glasses of water a day. Note: your food will digest better if you drink your water 1/2 hour *before* or one hour *after* a meal.

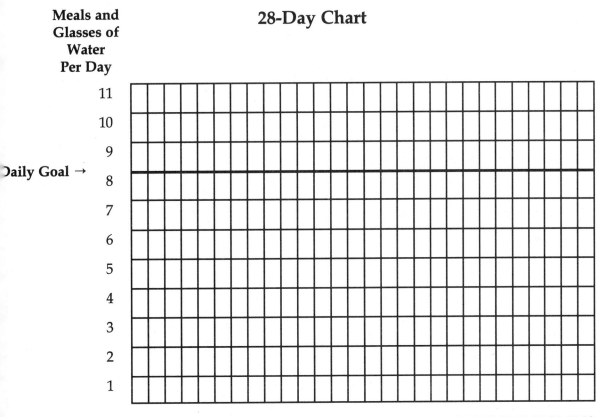

WHAT ABOUT THE MISSING DAYS? Read on!

HEART HEALTH

We can look at heart health from two perspectives; (1) how to have a healthy heart, and (2) how to avoid dying from heart disease. Both angles are covered in this section. The goal isn't to scare people. Neither is it to sugar-coat a serious topic.

You may ask yourself, how serious is coronary heart disease? Is there a chance that it will affect you or someone close to you? It's a major issue that presents the medical community with serious challenges. Consider the following:

1. Coronary heart disease is the number one cause of death in the Western world.
2. One-third of all heart attacks end in death (one-half of all first attacks).
3. Nearly twice as many people die from heart disease as from all kinds of cancer.
4. Sometimes heart disease presents no warning symptons.

Is your heart affected by how you live? You may disregard this as a serious question. All of us, at one time or another, discount the link between what we do and the resulting effect on our body and mind. Is the link between lifestyle and heart health real? You bet it is! Our lifestyle determines our probability of having trouble with heart disease. It's true that the genes we get from our parents and grandparents also help determine our heart health. If heart disease runs in the family, you should be extra careful about those risk factors that you can control.

RISK FACTORS YOU CAN CONTROL:

- Hypertension (high blood pressure)

- Cholesterol levels (ratio of total cholesterol to HDL)

- Smoking

- Sedentary lifestyle

- Obesity

- Stress

- Drug use and abuse

HOW TO HAVE A HEALTHY HEART

Heart disease is more prevalent in the Western world than in non-Western cultures which have a lower incidence of heart disease. Certain countries may enjoy more riches and comforts, but that does not protect the population from becoming ill. People in poorer countries often die sooner, but it's usually not from heart disease.

For example, in Asia, Africa, and South America, heart disease is far below that of the United States. Far fewer people in these cultures die from heart attack than America. This is no lucky accident. It reflects their "heart healthier" lifestyle. Lacking the West's high standard of living, Asians, Africans, and South Americans eat far less meat and cheese. They therefore have cleaner arteries—and fewer heart attacks. And because the automobile is often a luxury in these areas, people are forced to get more exercise by walking or cycling.

There is plenty you can do to protect your heart. The American Heart Association recommends the following changes in our diet to reduce our chances of suffering from coronary heart disease. You are advised to:

- Reduce saturated fat.
- Increase use of unsaturated fat (especially from cold-water fish).
- Reduce low density lipoproteins (LDLs) to under 125 mg a day.
- Gradually cut overall fat intake in half (the average in Western cultures is 40 percent of the diet—it needs to be cut to 20 percent.)
- Increase fiber consumption (especially from fruits and vegetables).

The exercise and nutrition sections of this book will assist you in meeting the above guidelines. Other sections of the book support the mental attitude and lifetime habits needed to continue meeting the guidelines.

In addition to recommendations for a healthy diet, the Heart Association feels that consumers need something they can trust when it comes to reading labels on food items. The Heart Guide program proposes a program where manufacturers purchase the right to display the "heart healthy" label on their products that meet the guidelines. These guidelines are that the food must be low in salt, cholesterol and fat.

The next page lists four control points you can use to keep your heart healthy and minimize the negative influence other factors may have on your heart.

FOUR STEPS TO A HEALTHY HEART: MAJOR CONTROL POINTS

CONTROL POINT 1: EXERCISE

An active lifestyle is a winning lifestyle. Forget reports of athletes who overdo it and have heart attacks. Research proves that people who maintain active lifestyles have fewer health problems than people who are sedentary. If a 50-year-old accountant has a heart attack while jogging, the reason is probably not because he's jogging but because he hasn't been jogging enough. The problem is more in the sudden nature of the lifestyle change than the exercise. A gradual transition into a healthy lifestyle is what this book is about.

- Be active every day.
- Combine socializing with active events.
- Make gradual, long-lasting changes.

CONTROL POINT 2: LIFE PRESSURE

Each of us experiences pressures and strains in our life. The decision people must make is whether or not to let the anxieties of life take over and control them. Every situation can be perceived as either ''stressful'' or ''challenging.'' Some people see life as a series of catastrophes. Those who manage stress best use terms like *challenge, adventure, task at hand,* or some other positive variation. This attitude is one of coping—rather than being afraid of losing or of being harmed.

- Attach positive labels to tough situations.
- Don't feel guilty about relaxing and enjoying a healthy lifestyle.
- Think ahead. Visualize pressure situations before you have to deal with them.

---

* For an excellent book on stress, order *Mental Fitness* by Merrill Raber using the information in the back of this book.

CONTROL POINT 3: NUTRITION

Your body can only work with what you put into it. Nutrition is an important factor in heart health. A good, balanced diet will keep your heart healthy. A diet should include the four food groups, and be low in saturated fats and cholesterol. If you have a condition such as hypertension, or if you have a family history of heart disease, your physician should be involved. He or she will be able to suggest various dietary alternatives, additions, drugs, or supplements. But most of us will do fine by eating moderate and balanced meals. There is no need to become a ''nuts and twigs'' fanatic. It's okay to give in to our vices from time to time. We're talking lifetime habits. We need to balance good eating with reasonable flexibility to leave room for socializing and enjoying life.

Remember:

- Eat well.
- Don't be a fanatic, be moderate.
- Start by shopping well.

CONTROL POINT 4: MENTAL ATTITUDE

Athletes in competition know that the mental game may be up to 80 percent of their success. A balanced attitude* considers the positive outcome of situations. Television, newspapers, and unhappy people expose us to negatives. Cutting down on negative inputs leaves room for the positive to blossom.

How does this relate to your heart? Doctors and therapists tell us that positive people get sick less often. When they do become ill, they recover more quickly and fully. Try some of the following suggestions:

- Close the door on the negative.
- Focus on solutions and progress toward goals.
- Take time to look for the positive.

Some people inherit a predisposition to coronary heart disease. In this case, your mental attitude is even more important in combating the negative pressures and feelings and helplessness.

Personal Wellness

---

* Order *Attitude: Your Most Priceless Possession* using the information in the back of this book.

21 WAYS TO A HEALTHY HEART

Read at this list from two angles. First, put a check mark next to the good things you are already doing. Second, check a few improvement areas that you can realistically include in your regular routine.

MY HEART AGENDA	I'm doing this already.	I intend to start doing this today.
1. Avoid sudden changes in your physical activity or lifestyle.	☐	☐
2. Schedule regular medical checkups.	☐	☐
3. Know the signs of heart attack.	☐	☐
4. Understand the causes of heart disease.	☐	☐
5. Become familiar with your family history of disease and heart attacks.	☐	☐
6. Avoid prolonged stressful situations.	☐	☐
7. Avoid intensive stressful situations.	☐	☐
8. Take action to lower your stress level.	☐	☐
9. Eat a balanced diet: plenty of fruits, vegetables, and whole grains.	☐	☐
10. Reduce the total amount of fat in your diet.	☐	☐
11. Avoid fats that become hard at room temperature (saturated fats).	☐	☐
12. Reduce the amount of red meat you eat. This will lower cholesterol and fat levels.	☐	☐
13. Do some low-level activity every day.	☐	☐
14. Do moderate to vigorous physical activity 3–4 times a week.	☐	☐
15. Never exercise or work so hard that you feel dizzy, sweat profusely, and can't breathe.	☐	☐
16. Always check out any sign of heart problems. Don't be embarrassed that it may be a false alarm.	☐	☐
17. Stop smoking! Consult your physician and enter a smoking cessation program.	☐	☐
18. Read the labels on all food items. Watch for sodium, saturated fats, and sugar.	☐	☐
19. Have your blood pressure and cholesterol measured regularly.	☐	☐
20. Read up on current medical tests and information. Stay informed.	☐	☐
21. Relax, take it easy, and enjoy the life you've worked so hard to build.	☐	☐

HEART ATTACK SIGNS

The difference between full recovery and permanent damage during a heart attack is often a matter of minutes. The number of minutes between the beginning of the heart attack and getting medical attention can make the difference between life and death. Precious minutes are wasted when the victim denies that the signs and symptoms might actually indicate a heart attack.

Following are some of the signs and symptoms to watch for:

- Chest pain or tightness
- Dizziness
- Spreading pain to shoulders, neck, jaw, arms, or back
- Feeling faint
- Sweating
- Pale, ashen look

With current medications and treatments, damage can be prevented if you get help quickly, especially during the first four hours. It's better to risk a false alarm and possible embarrassment than to sit back and wait, hoping the pain and discomfort will simply go away.

Caution: Many people suffer heart attacks each year without experiencing any signs of trouble. Others notice one or two of the symptoms in a mild form.

Should You Be Tested? It is a good idea to know about tests to check on heart health. Ask your physician which are most appropriate for you and your family:

- Heart risk factor analysis
- Stress test
- Blood pressure test
- Blood lipids test (cholesterol, triglycerides, blood sugar)
- EKG (electrocardiogram)

Wellness Affirmation

HEART HEALTH: What I do affects my heart. I control my level of stress, eating, drinking, smoking and exercising so that my heart functions well. I believe in moderation. My doctor and my balanced lifestyle combine to keep my heart heathly and strong.

MY CARDIOVASCULAR INVENTORY*

In the space next to each item, write *Yes, No,* or *Sometimes.*

1. I have regular medical checkups   _____

2. I have specific heart checkups   _____

3. I have a balanced diet   _____

4. I exercise moderately   _____

5. I exercise consistently   _____

6. I control my stress   _____

7. I maintain a low cholesterol level   _____

8. I relax regularly   _____

9. I have no family history of heart disease   _____

10. I pace myself well   _____

Your Score
> 8–10 Yes's: Keep it up!
> 6–7 Yes's: OK, but not very safe.
> 5 Yes's or Less: Very risky. Make changes and see your doctor!

Wellness Affirmation

POSITIVE ATTITUDE: My attitude is great. People are basically good and life can be very sweet. If I look, the world has amazing amounts of good things happening all the time. I avoid negative people, articles and news stories. I'm realistic but very positive.

---

* From the book *Professional Balance,* by Rick Griggs. For more information, contact Crisp Publications, Inc., 95 First Street, Los Altos, CA 94022.

PART II

CONTROLLING THE UNHEALTHY CULPRITS

CHOLESTEROL

"SLUDGE THAT GUMS THE SYSTEM"

Cholesterol is a white, waxy substance produced naturally by the body when it digests certain foods such as cheese, butter, eggs, and red meat. Atherosclerosis, or hardening of the arteries, is often the result of too much cholesterol from too much fat and not enough exercise. Atheroslerosis results in heart attacks, blood clots, and strokes.

Cholesterol is a major part of the problem. A one percent drop in your total cholesterol will result in a two percent reduction in your chances of developing heart disease according to the National Heart, Lung, and Blood Institute.

As with most aspects of life, there is a good side and a bad side to cholesterol. The good part is the HDLs (high-density lipoproteins), which seem to remove excess cholesterol from the bloodstream and tissue cells.

The bad cholesterol, the LDLs (low-density lipoproteins), carry excess cholesterol that builds up as fatty deposits inside the arteries. It's very probable that some of the 1.5 million heart attacks and the 500,000 deaths in America each year result from the battle between the good HDLs and the dastardly LDLs.

Recent studies suggest that low levels of HDLs in the blood, combined with a high cholesterol reading, can also increase the risk of heart disease. An overall cholesterol level below 200 is great. The next step is to check on the ratio of total cholesterol to HDL.

Women entering menopause should be aware that LDL levels typically shoot up about 12 points. To make matters worse, HDL levels tend to drop about four points. This makes it more important for women to understand and control other factors in their lives that influence cholesterol levels.

There are two ways cholesterol ends up in your bloodstream. It is manufactured naturally by the liver; and it is found in certain foods, such as animal fat, butter, cheese, and eggs. You can't do much about the cholesterol your liver makes. But you can control what you eat. There's still some controversy about the importance of a low-fat, low-cholesterol diet for maintaining cardiovascular health, but the American Heart Association stands by its dietary recommendations.

Naturally, large and small firms have been quick to hop on the health-food bandwagon. Oat bran, for example, is available in many forms. But it is valuable to know that fruit and vegetables are also good sources of fiber.

Animal products contain cholesterol. Plant products do not.

MORE ABOUT CHOLESTEROL

CHOLESTEROL: WHAT TO DO.

Following are some steps that will help you get and keep cholesterol under control. Check the ones you're already doing. Then check the ones you plan to start doing.

MY CHOLESTEROL STRATEGY	I'm doing this already.	I intend to start doing this today.
1. Control hypertension (blood pressure).	☐	☐
2. Have your cholesterol levels checked regularly.	☐	☐
3. Reduce dietary intake of saturated fats. (Saturated fats are solid at room temperature).	☐	☐
4. Exercise moderately and consistently.	☐	☐
5. Include plenty of fiber in your diet (oats, fruits, vegetables).	☐	☐
6. Keep total cholesterol under 200 mg a day.	☐	☐
7. Keep LDL cholesterol near 125.	☐	☐
8. Eat low-to-moderate amounts of animal fat, butter, cheese, eggs, and liver.	☐	☐

WHAT NUMBERS SHOULD I WATCH? To lower the risk of coronary heart disease keep an eye on these amounts:

Total cholesterol: under 200 mg a day is low risk.
LDL: 125–185 is moderate risk. Over 185 is high risk.
HDL: below 35 is moderate risk.

The ratio of total cholesterol to HDL should be about 4:1. Remember: *You want to keep LDL down and HDL up.* Most of the recommendations in this book will help you with one or both of these goals. Keep reading!

TOTAL CHOLESTEROL = HDL + LDL + VLDL
(high-density + low-density + very low density lipoproteins)

SMOKING

Most people have tried smoking at one time or another. It may have been a one-time experiment in elementary school, a way to gain popularity in high school, or an attempt to reduce nervous tension on the job.

If you smoke, or know others who do, you are aware of how hard it is to change the habit. Smoking isn't an isolated behavior. It's mixed in with eating, drinking, working, socializing, and driving. It is difficult to quit smoking, but there are some absolute benefits. The biggest is that nonsmokers and former smokers have a 52 percent lower death rate from coronary heart disease than smokers have. This is great news because it indicates that the risk of heart disease can be greatly modified by quitting.

Cataracts are another malady connected to smoking. Smoking seems to be related to an increase in nuclear cataracts. These are the ones that occur inside of the lens of the eye, causing the lens to become cloudy. An interesting finding among the same group found that the number of cortical cataracts (outside the lens) was not reduced by quitting smoking—but it was reduced by wearing sunglasses and hats.

Well, there it is again. We keep finding that the way we live and the things we do affect whether we get sick or stay healthy. Wearing hats and sunglasses is easy. Eliminating an addictive nicotine habit is a lot harder.

What does the dictionary say about nicotine? ''A poisonous alkaloid derived from the tobacco plant, used in medicine and as an insecticide.''

''Tobacco surely was designed to poison and destroy mankind.'' —Philip Freneau

The next few pages will give you some useful facts about smoking. See how much you really know about this subject. Take the ''smoking quizzes'' and check how well you scored.

SMOKING AND WELLNESS (continued)

CAN A SMOKER REALLY QUIT?

Are you one of those smokers who has tried to quit over and over? Maybe you've seen someone close to you make attempt after attempt to give up cigarettes. Smoking is one of the most addictive habits known. The longer you continue, the more difficult it is to break the habit.

SMOKING QUIZ 1: How Many Smokers Quit and Start Again?

- ☐ 10%
- ☐ 20%
- ☐ 30%
- ☐ 40%
- ☐ 50%
- ☐ 60%

Yes, you can quit—and not start again. Keep reading, and start a 28-day smoking chart (you'll find it in a few pages).

SMOKING QUIZ 2: How Many Smokers (over age 20) Are There In The United States?

- ☐ 10 million
- ☐ 20 million
- ☐ 30 million
- ☐ 40 million
- ☐ 50 million
- ☐ 60 million

Smoking has steadily decreased in most segments of the population. (Two segments where smoking hasn't decreased significantly are among minorities and teenagers.)

SMOKING QUIZ 3: Women Who Smoke ''Low-Yield'' Cigarettes Are How Many Times More Likely To Have a First Heart Attack Than Women Who Don't Smoke?

- ☐ equally likely
- ☐ twice as likely
- ☐ 3 times more likely
- ☐ 4 times more likely
- ☐ 5 times more likely
- ☐ 6 times more likely

All cigarette smokers have a greater risk of heart attacks.

SMOKING QUIZ 4: Are These Statements True Or False?

1. ☐ T ☐ F Smoking is the chief avoidable cause of death.
2. ☐ T ☐ F More people die from smoking than from auto accidents, AIDS, and suicide combined.
3. ☐ T ☐ F About 10 million people a year try to quit smoking.
4. ☐ T ☐ F Tobacco companies have your best interest in mind.
5. ☐ T ☐ F Smoking significantly affects cholesterol levels.
6. ☐ T ☐ F Low-nicotine cigarettes make smoking safe.
7. ☐ T ☐ F Lung cancer death rates among men are beginning to fall.
8. ☐ T ☐ F Smoking is so addictive it's almost impossible to quit.
9. ☐ T ☐ F If you've smoked for many years, quitting now won't help much.
10. ☐ T ☐ F Improving in other wellness areas gives momentum and incentives to quit smoking.

Lung disease is declining as smoking rates are reduced, especially in the Western states. The Centers for Disease Control report that smoking caused 28 lung-disease deaths per 100,000 population in Hawaii and 87 per 100,000 in Wyoming.

What's the cause: sun, moon, television, sports...or could it be our lifestyle?

In 1985, 30 percent of the adult population smoked. In 1987 it was down to 29 percent. The goal for 1990 is: under 25 percent.

Answers:
Smoking Quiz 1: 40 percent of smokers quit and start again.
Smoking Quiz 2: There are 48.8 million adult smokers in the United States.
Smoking Quiz 3: Women who smoke low-yield cigarettes are four times more likely to have a heart attack than women who don't smoke (Source: *American Health*).

Smoking Quiz 4:
1. True. Quitting smoking has a major impact on health and longevity.
2. True. 390,000 people die in the United States each year from smoking-related causes.
3. False. 17.3 million try at least 1 day a year.
4. False. Their interest is in profits and survival.
5. True. One cigarette raises total cholesterol by about 1/2 point.
6. False. Smoking low or regular nicotine brands more than triples the risk of heart attack, compared to not smoking at all.
7. True. Lung cancer deaths among men who stopped smoking are beginning to fall.
8. False. People quit every single day.
9. False. Quitting now will significantly reduce your risk of suffering a heart attack.
10. True. Many former smokers connect quitting smoking with other healthy habits.

SMOKING AND CHOLESTEROL

We've already said a lot of bad things about cholesterol. Well, here's a bit more information:

1 cigarette = 1/2 points gained in total cholesterol

The *American Heart Journal* reports that when several thousand men and women under the age of 50 were tested, some shocking links were found between smoking and total cholesterol levels.

Increase in Total Cholesterol

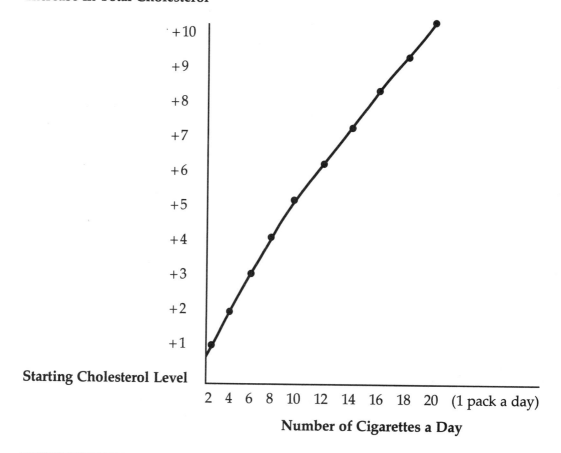

Starting Cholesterol Level

Number of Cigarettes a Day

Source: *American Heart Journal.* Men and women under age 50. 55,000 people screened.

If you smoke and have high cholesterol, you are encouraged to seek professional help in controlling how much you smoke.

SMOKING AND CAFFEINE

Smoking is also associated with other life-threatening conditions, such as house fires, grass fires, and auto accidents. It's deadly by itself, and even worse in combination with other risk factors such as obesity, hypertension, stress, family history of heart disease, and poor nutrition. Can you think of any good reasons to continue smoking?

HOW ABOUT CAFFEINE?

Smoking and coffee seem to go together. The tar in cigarette smoke speeds up the liver's metabolism of caffeine—so if you quit smoking, more caffeine will stay in your blood stream. This can lead to more nervousness and sleeplessness, which in turn will aggravate your withdrawal symptoms and make it more difficult for you to quit.

Caffeine raises your heart rate, urine production, and general metabolism. Excessive consumption (over 750 milligrams a day) leads to a condition known as caffeinism. One large cup of coffee has about 200 milligrams of caffeine. A safe dose of caffeine is 200 milligrams a day.

   5 oz of coffee contains 150 mg of caffeine.
   5 oz of tea contains 50 mg of caffeine.
   5 oz of soft drink contains under 50 mg of caffeine.
   5 oz of milk chocolate contains 30 mg of caffeine.
   1 oz of baking chocolate contains 35 mg of caffeine.

28-DAY SMOKING CHARTS

These two 28-day smoking charts are tools to make your progress visible and rewarding. Use them as positive tools for ongoing improvement in your life. When they become a chore, or a source of guilt, toss them.

Start today or tomorrow. Begin with an easy, achievable goal, and to be consistent, fill it out at the same time each day.

**Number of
Cigarettes
Per Day**

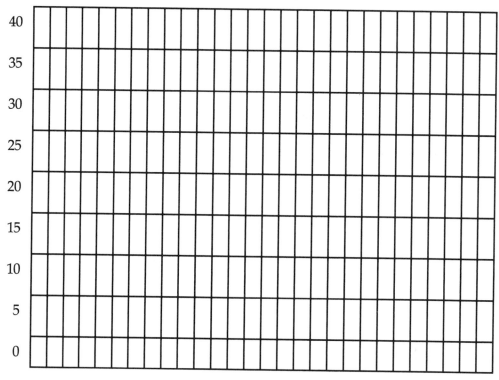

Cutting Down

Days of Success

GOAL = A downward trend

QUITTING COMPLETELY

Number of Consecutive Hours Without Smoking

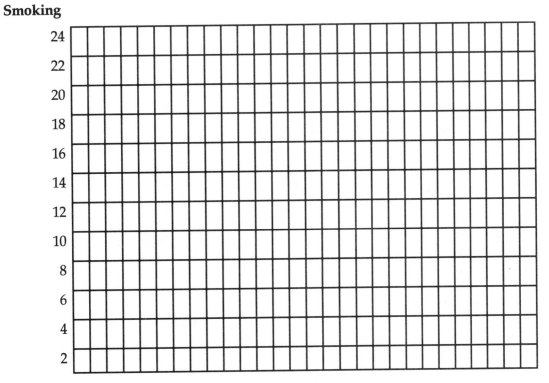

Quitting Completely

Days of Success

SMOKING AND WELLNESS (continued)

Wellness Affirmation

CURRENTLY SMOKING: I have the power to cut down on my cigarette smoking and eventually quit. I am getting better control over my life habits. Smoking is one habit I am able to control. As time goes by I am getting better and better control over my smoking.

IS SMOKELESS TOBACCO SAFE?

One in five male college students have used smokeless tobacco.

Snuff and chew (smokeless tobacco) users absorb twice as much nicotine as cigarette smokers. Some research has found that these tobacco substitutes increase blood pressure and heart rate. Records show that this top choice of most baseball players (snuff, chewing tobacco) produces precancerous oral lesions.

Wellness Affirmation

QUIT SMOKING: I am no longer a smoker. Count me as one of the success stories. I already see that the benefits far outnumber the temporary difficulties. My life is cleaner, healthier, and much more positive. I have complete control over the habits in my life.

ALCOHOL AND DRUGS

Let's start this section by answering a few questions. Believe it or not, you already have definite opinions and attitudes about using drugs or drinking alcohol.

Check the items below that you tend to *agree* with. I feel it is OK to:

- ☐ Occasionally drink
- ☐ Drink alone
- ☐ Drink alcohol with meals
- ☐ Have 1–2 drinks per day
- ☐ Drink every day
- ☐ Never drink
- ☐ Smoke marijuana at parties
- ☐ Never smoke marijuana
- ☐ Smoke marijuana at home
- ☐ Smoke marijuana in the car
- ☐ Smoke marijuana at concerts
- ☐ Use cocaine at parties
- ☐ Rarely use cocaine
- ☐ Never use cocaine
- ☐ Occasionally use other drugs/chemicals
- ☐ Use drugs/chemicals only at parties
- ☐ Never use drugs/chemicals

It is important to understand how you feel about substance use and abuse. An overall term, chemical dependency, applies to the chronic situation where a person uses a substance to the point where it interferes with an important part of their life.

CHEMICALS

Chemicals include alcohol, depressants, opiates, perceptual distorters (LSD), and stimulants. The pattern of use and abuse usually follows a predictable cycle from occasional use, increased use, work/family tension, increased use, work/family disruption, loss of control, attempts at recovery, and unfortunately like many other illnesses, eventually it can lead to death.

ALCOHOL AND DRUGS: USE AND ABUSE

Where does it end? Can you drink or do drugs a little and not get into trouble? A lot of drug and alcohol abuse started at a stage where it was moderate and controlled. For a variety of reasons, usage often progresses to a stage where it is used intensely. The person gradually loses control over the use. When this happens it begins to affect life in more obvious and troublesome ways.

Place an X on the scale where you personally feel it is safe to be. In each case the *left* side will lean towards the conservative side and the *right* will be on the permissive side.

TOTAL ABSTINENCE	CONTROLLED USE
NEVER TOUCH IT	TRY EVERYTHING ONCE
AVOID ALL USERS	JOIN IN WITH FRIENDS
NO DRINKS WHEN DRIVING	A FEW IS FINE
NEVER USE IT AT WORK	DURING BREAKS IS OK

ALCOHOL QUIZ:

1. ☐ T ☐ F You get less drunk on beer and wine than on hard liquor.
2. ☐ T ☐ F 50% of all traffic fatalities involve alcohol.
3. ☐ T ☐ F 10% of the workforce are active alcoholics.
4. ☐ T ☐ F Alcoholics are usually minorities and street people.
5. ☐ T ☐ F Professional businesspeople often lose control of alcohol.
6. ☐ T ☐ F Recovering alcoholics can drink moderately.
7. ☐ T ☐ F Combining alcohol and drugs is deadly.
8. ☐ T ☐ F Alcohol increases the chance of having an accident.
9. ☐ T ☐ F Alcohol is suspected in several types of cancers.
10. ☐ T ☐ F Teenage auto fatalities usually involve alcohol.

Answers: 1, 4 and 6 are false, the rest are true.

ALCOHOL AND DRUGS KILL IN TWO (2) STAGES

Alcohol costs millions of victims their lives. During adolescence, alcohol and drugs kill as a result of traffic accidents. Later in life alcohol and drugs kill from chronic diseases such as cirrhosis of the liver and hepatitis, cancers and digestive diseases.

SIGNS OF DRUG ABUSE

Now that you've reviewed your feelings and attitudes on alcohol and drugs, you may wonder if it is any of your business to get involved in other people's lives when they seem to have alcohol and/or drug problems. It may be a family member, a co-worker, a friend, spouse or lover. It is a tough call on when to intervene, but it's an absolute *must* to recognize the signs and symptoms of substance abuse and take appropriate action.

Following are some *possible* signs that someone may be using/abusing a substance to the point that it is affecting a major life activity. Individually, each symptom does not suggest substance abuse, but as a group or pattern, the probability is high.

FAMILY MEMBER

- change in eating habits
- excessive spending without something to ''show''
- more argumentative than normal
- less interaction with other family than normal
- unpredictable mood swings

CO-WORKER/EMPLOYEE:

- higher absenteeism than normal
- increased tardiness
- more sick-leave than usual
- unpredictable mood swings
- lower productivity
- more mistakes and accidents

FRIEND

- less social interaction than normal
- less participation in usual activities than normal
- physical illnesses and complaints
- unpredictable mood swings

---

* For more information on this topic, order *Job Performance and Chemical Dependency* using the information in the back of this book.

TREATMENT FOR ALCOHOL AND DRUG PROBLEMS

You've heard about them and even joked about them. You can probably name several celebrities who have entered alcohol and drug treatment programs. Sometimes our sense is that they are serious about their problem. At other times we get the impression that it's a publicity/legal maneuver.

Treatment programs can be short or long. They vary from a few weeks to several months. Many programs start out with an intensive *residential phase* where the individual lives at a center for a few weeks. This residential phase is followed by an *on-going phase*. Here is where the person continues the recovery support program while maintaining their usual work/home routine.

Outpatient programs are an option where the person attends evening and/or weekend sessions for about 4–5 weeks. This phase is also followed-up with on-going recovery services like the tail end of the residential programs.

Any program that attempts to change addictive behavior must be continued over time. The initial treatment should lead into a long process of building control, maintaining a support group, and resolving the usual life problems as they arise.

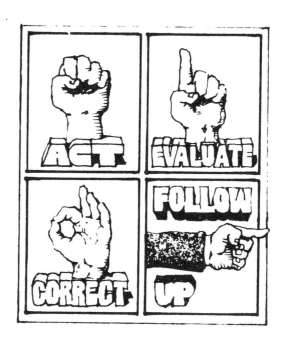

WEIGHT CONTROL

Just about everyone has tried to change their weight. Many young people want to put on weight to be better in certain sports. Others wish to take off weight to fit the image in a glamor magazine or to help fit in during those awkward high school years.

HOW DO YOU FEEL ABOUT YOUR SCALE WEIGHT?

Put a check mark next to the sentence that best describes your attitude.

☐ I weigh too little.

☐ I weigh just the right amount.

☐ I weigh too much.

☐ I never weigh myself (and don't want to).

☐ I'm afraid to weigh myself (but I want to).

Although the bathroom scale has some serious drawbacks, it does give you a first look at how you are controlling your weight. It is usually the first signal that you may need to alter some of the things you're doing.

PROBLEMS WITH THE BATHROOM SCALE

- It's not very accurate.
- It doesn't distinguish between fat and muscle.
- It doesn't allow for water retention.
- It gives a false sense of security.

Is there a better way to measure how well your wellness program is working? The following pages contain general alternatives.

WEIGHT CONTROL (Continued)

FORGET THE SCALE

Question: What is better than the bathroom scale?

Answers:
1. Underwater weighing
2. Caliper measures of body fat
3. Electrical impedance measures of body fat
4. Inches and clothes sizes

Following are brief descriptions of various ways to accurately check your weight control progress. A lot of people combine one or more of these methods with the bathroom scale in order to get a more complete picture of how much healthy body tissue is being exchanged for fat.

1. *Underwater weighing* gives one of the most accurate measures of how much fat there is on your body. You are strapped into a harness and lowered into a pool of water for a few seconds. Fat floats and muscle sinks. A higher underwater weight shows a higher ratio of muscle and bones to fat.

2. *Calipers* are used at two or three locations on the body to measure the amount of fat underneath the skin. This gives a rough estimate of the total percentage of fat in the body.

3. *Electrical impedance* measures fat in the body by testing how fast a small current will pass through the body. This gives another rough estimate of the amount of body fat the person has.

4. *Inches and clothes sizes* also give a picture of how much fat you have. They also tell how much muscle you are exchanging for fat. Fat takes more space than muscle. If you are exercising 3–4 times a week, you will notice your inches dropping while your scale weight may stay the same. The new, healthy muscle tissue may weigh as much as the fat you are losing, but it takes up less space.

BODY FAT AND MUSCLE

Body fat is not just that bulge you can see in the mirror. It is also the fat that hides inside your muscles and in between muscles and organs. Twin sisters can have identical scale weight but a dramatic difference in body fat. They might even look the same and wear the same clothes, but the ''inside story'' may be very different.

Pamela eats well and likes to play sports. She doesn't overdo it, but stays healthy and eats good food. Her twin sister Ruth hates to exercise, so she diets to stay as slim as Pamela. Ruth is on a diet most of the time. She often splurges on weekends, then on Monday and Tuesday she may only eat two meals.

Ruth and Pamela went to a health faire where they had a water weighing tank for measuring body fat. Pamela wanted to get weighed. Ruth didn't care for it but agreed to finally settle the matter over which lifestyle really kept the weight off. Ruth had always bragged that she could party a lot, and still be as healthy as her ''jock'' sister.

The results were amazing. Pamela had a body fat percentage of 16. Ruth's came out at 33 percent body fat. She couldn't believe that a full one-third of her body was fat. The twins played a lot more tennis together after that health faire.

These twins aren't the only ones who are surprised when they find how much of their body is fat. The exchange of fat for healthy tissue is a continuing battle. When muscles aren't used, they atrophy, or shrink. When this happens, calories are stored as fat. If your diet doesn't change as you become more sedentary, your body fat percentage will increase.

Let's take another look at how your weight can stay the same while the ratio of muscle to fat begins to change.

In high school, Joel weighed 157 pounds. He played soccer and basketball and ran some track after school. Years later he weighs exactly the same, and yet he doesn't exercise. The only sports he sees are on the tube and his most strenuous activity is between the refrigerator and the couch.

What do you think?

Is anything wrong with Joel's situation?

Can Joel trust his bathroom scale?

How do you think Joel's high school clothes would fit today?

There is something wrong with Joel's situation. It's the false sense of security he receives from his scale weight. His body is deteriorating and his percentage of fat is probably double what it was in high school. This puts extra pressure on his heart and blood vessels.

WATER AND WEIGHT CONTROL

Water works wonders for controlling weight. If you can make it a point to drink five to eight glasses of water every day, you'll have a powerful weight control tool on your side. Water rids the body of stored fat. Your kidneys need plenty of water to function. When you don't drink enough water, your kidneys become less efficient. They pass some of their work off to the liver.

HOW BIG ARE THESE GLASSES ANYWAY?

You need to drink five to eight glasses of water a day—but what size glasses? Check the size you think is meant.

☐ 6-ounce glasses
☐ 8-ounce glasses
☐ 10-ounce glasses
☐ 12-ounce glasses (size of a soft drink can)
☐ 14-ounce glasses
☐ 16-ounce glasses

The answer is five to eight 8-oz glasses—or two and 1/2 to four 16-oz glasses.

IS WATER REALLY THAT HELPFUL?

Definitely yes. If you can include those five to eight glasses a day your body benefits in several ways:

- Fluid retention—You have to drink water to eliminate water.
- Obesity—Being overweight raises the need for more water.
- Muscle tone—Water helps muscle contraction and avoids dehydration.
- Skin tone—Water helps eliminate the sagging during weight loss.
- Waste removal—Water flushes out the metabolized fat during weight loss.
- Constipation—Adequate water reduces the need to siphon it from the colon.

Remember, your liver metabolizes fat. When the kidneys don't have enough water to do their job they steal time from the liver. So keep drinking that water to help your kidneys, liver, and weight control.

SET POINT

Researchers believe that each person has a normal weight that the body tries to maintain, called a set point. This is why diets don't work. As soon as a person diets, the body begins storing fat and lowering its metabolism. When the diet is over, the weight is quickly gained back and you're back to your original set point.

THE UPS AND DOWNS OF DIETING

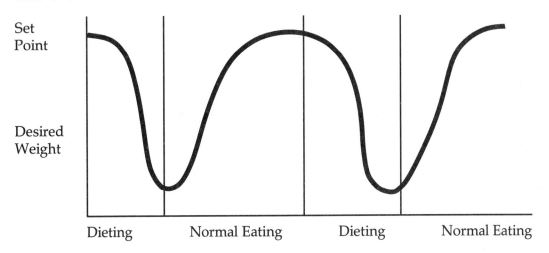

A more successful approach is to change your set point. With good nutrition, moderate exercise, and gradual weight loss you will permanently lower your natural set point.

A BETTER METHOD OF WEIGHT CONTROL

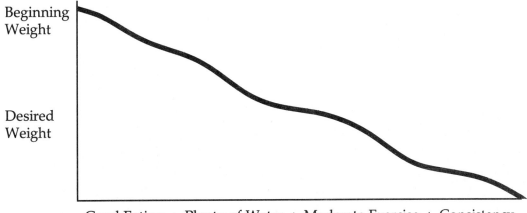

HOW DO YOU JUGGLE CALORIES?

The calorie juggling act gets played out in some strange ways. Some people hope to lose weight by not eating. Others are exercise fanatics and can't get enough physical activity. Still others, in extreme cases, eat and then force themselves to throw up. All of these have some serious problems.

You'll do better at controlling your weight if you have a good understanding of caloric balance. But first, note that

---

ONE POUND OF FAT
= 3500 CALORIES

CALORIC BALANCE

Caloric balance means that you burn off the same number of calories that you take in. If you take in 4,000 or even 8,000 calories a day and burn the same amount, your scale weight will remain constant.

Think of your body as a long water tank with openings on the two ends. Water (like calories) enters at one end, and exits at the other. There are two ways to maintain the ideal size of the tank: take in less water at one end, or let more out at the other. Your body isn't a tank, but the basic idea of taking in less and burning more is the best method of weight control.

Control of your caloric balance will help you maintain ideal weight, or move in the right direction towards your goals.

Wellness Affirmation

WEIGHT CONTROL: I no longer diet because I understand caloric balance. Weight control means equalizing the calories taken in with those being burned off. I aim for my ideal weight with a combination of good eating, moderation, and consistent exercising. I never lose more than 2–3 pounds a week.

STRESS

All of us have stress in our lives. Some of us have too little, others have too much. One person may suffer and get sick from stress, while another seems to thrive on the challenge and adventure. What's the difference? How can people in similar situations react to them so differently?

Stress is the nonspecific response of the mind and body to any real or perceived demands placed on them. In other words, whenever there is a demand on your body, or you think there is a demand, your whole being kicks into high gear and prepares to fight back or run away. Stress comes more from your perception of demands than from the actual events.

You have a choice in how you label a situation. Some take the negative, stressful angle. Others lean toward the positive, challenging angle.

WHERE DO YOU FIT IN?

Check the statement that best describes you:

☐ I have too little pressure in my life.

☐ I have too much pressure in my life.

☐ I have just the right amount of pressure in my life.

Your health is directly affected by the stress you encounter and your reaction to it. There are two connections between stress and good health.

CONNECTION 1   High stress leads to poor health.

CONNECTION 2   Good health leads to higher tolerance for stress.

Keep reading for a closer look at whether you have too little or too much pressure in your life.

HOW MUCH PRESSURE CAN YOU TAKE?

1. TOO LITTLE PRESSURE

This situation is just having too little to do. The boredom, confusion, and frustration of not being able to perform seems to lead to stress. Quite often, employees will list boredom as a main cause of their stress at work. Informal surveys during stress management classes show that people prefer too much work to too little. People want and need to be busy and active.

2. TOO MUCH PRESSURE

This situation is an overwhelming sense of being out of control. The pressures, demands, and duties of work and home life add up to heavy stress. It all depends on how we interpret or perceive events.

WHAT DO YOU SAY TO YOURSELF

PERCEPTION 1 Pressure means trouble, problems, and fear.

PERCEPTION 2 Pressure is a challenge that calls for coping and perhaps some hard work.

3. JUST THE RIGHT AMOUNT

This is paradise—where you've got enough pressure in your life and work to keep you alert and challenged. You're up for the battle and you even welcome it.

"OF ALL THE TROUBLES RUMBLING DOWN THE ROAD STRAIGHT FOR YOU...MOST OF THEM WILL END UP IN THE DITCH BEFORE GETTING TO YOU."

NOTE: For an excellent book on stress, order *Mental Fitness* using the information in the back of this book. A video based on this book titled *Stress and Mental Fitness* is also available. For more information, please contact Crisp Publications.

WHAT CAUSES STRESS?

Where does stress come from? Stress can come from money, health, or work problems. Stress can even come from positive changes in your life like promotions, new babies, and extra money.

WHAT CAUSES STRESS IN YOUR WORK LIFE?

Check any of the areas that apply to your life at work.

☐ Boss   ☐ Peers   ☐ Employees

☐ Meetings   ☐ Writing   ☐ Salary

☐ Commuting   ☐ Layoffs   ☐ Family pressures

☐ Traveling   ☐ Other _____   ☐ Other _____

WHERE DOES STRESS COME FROM IN YOUR HOME LIFE?

Check any of the areas that apply to your home, family, and personal life.

☐ Relatives   ☐ Community obligations   ☐ Classes

☐ Spouse   ☐ Illness   ☐ Finances

☐ Health   ☐ Work pressures   ☐ Sexual problems

☐ Children   ☐ Other _____   ☐ Other _____

Take a few minutes to think about those areas of your life that cause you stress. A good approach would be to verify the ones you checked to see if they actually raise your stress level. The next step is to explore your perception of that part of your life. You might make progress just by looking at it from a positive and challenging angle. Start by picking three good aspects of each area that you checked as a cause of stress.

STRESS: A CASE STUDY

A HEALTHY NURSE

Here's a person who knows where stress comes from. The nurse in the case below has a tough schedule but remembers the two connections between stress and health. She also knows that stress comes from her perception of events rather than the events themselves.

Beverly is a registered nurse. She works a night shift, but tries to keep a reasonable exercise and eating schedule during times she isn't working. Sometimes she'd rather get more sleep—but remembers times she stopped exercising. Her life missed "something" and she never felt "100%" when she didn't work out. She is convinced that her tough schedule (including day classes) will work only if she stays with her moderate exercise and nutrition program.

Beverly doesn't touch red meat or fatty foods. She goes out with her friends and gets wild once in a while, but always tries to squeeze in some biking, jogging, or tennis. She's not fanatical about her exercise, so she doesn't get angry or upset when she misses a session or two. But she swears that she feels different if she misses more than two exercise sessions or eats too much junk food. Beverly has learned that to manage her stress, it's easier to stay on a healthy schedule than to try getting back on a strict schedule.

Have you noticed that some people just handle things well and rarely seem stressed out? What do these people have, and how can you get it?

THE STRESS-RESISTANT PERSON

Dr. Raymond B. Flannery, Jr., studied people who seldom became ill, never missed appointments or classes, and seemed in control of their lives. Here are the characteristics he found:

1. They took personal control and responsibility over events in their lives.
2. They were committed to a goal.
3. They used few substances or chemicals and were active in their lives.
4. They had strong social bonds to other people.

REDUCING STRESS

You've already picked probable sources of your stress. Now let's look at some easy ways of reducing the pressure and anxiety of your life.

AT WORK

Check any of the areas that help reduce stress in your work or career life.

☐ Meetings	☐ Friends	☐ Vacations
☐ Traveling	☐ Accomplishments	☐ Exercising
☐ Lunch Breaks	☐ Walking	☐ Reading
☐ Special Projects	☐ Other _____	☐ Other _____

AT HOME

Check any of the areas that help reduce stress in your home, family, or personal life.

☐ Vacations	☐ Meal times	☐ Eating out
☐ Spouse	☐ Socializing	☐ Exercising
☐ Walking	☐ Gardening	☐ Sex and romance
☐ Children	☐ Other _____	☐ Other _____

Your stress reducers will be different from those of others. It is important to find which ones have a positive effect in your work or home life. As you find and use the ones that are effective, you'll notice your life pressures will be more often at that good level that leads to high performance.

STRESS AND PERFORMANCE

This diagram shows the relation of stress level to performance. You can see that performance is low when stress is either too low or too high.

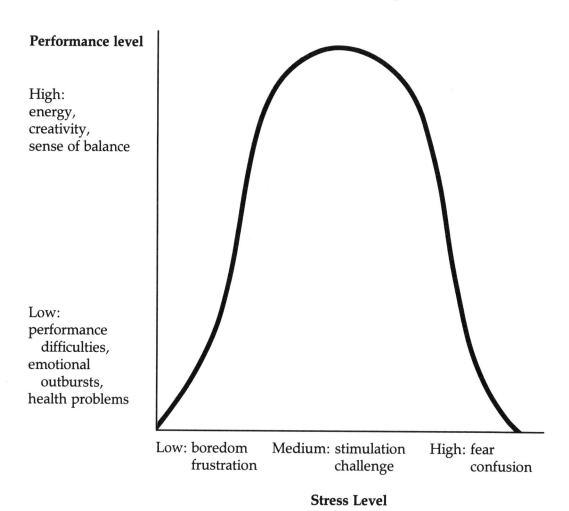

Performance level

High:
energy,
creativity,
sense of balance

Low:
performance
   difficulties,
emotional
   outbursts,
health problems

Low: boredom   Medium: stimulation   High: fear
   frustration   challenge   confusion

Stress Level

Do you see yourself at any level on this graph? You may find yourself at different places when you think of your work or personal life.

PRESSURE, STRESS & ANXIETY

A more accurate picture may be that performance starts low with low stress. The next area is the best. Here is where you are at your optimum performance level. Following the optimal performance level there will be a *gradual decrease,* or a sudden drop in your performance level.

STRESS AND PERFORMANCE

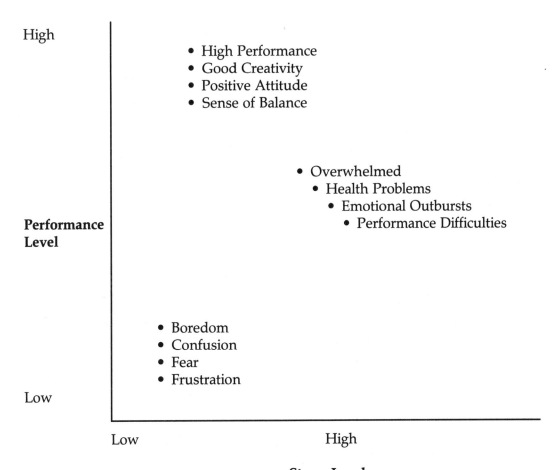

Keep in mind that good and bad things can move you from left to right on this scale and it's your *perception* of those good and bad events that ends up being translated into stress.

A CLOSE CALL

Can the way you *think* about things really affect your health and wellness? Read the following case.

A CLOSE CALL FOR JERRY

Jerry worked for the U.S. Navy for much of his career. When stationed in the San Francisco Bay Area he reported for duty at the Treasure Island Naval Station. This is on an island halfway across the Oakland–San Francisco Bridge.

The Navy review board was to rule on Jerry's rather complicated discharge situation. Jerry was worried about the outcome. The day before the review board was to make its decision, Jerry was heading home over the Bay Bridge. He began to feel nauseous and dizzy. He kept driving until he actually began to feel faint. He pulled over to the side of the road just as he began to pass out.

At the hospital they said Jerry had all the signs of a heart attack. They began their testing, hooked up an intravenous drip, and connected him to an EKG (heart monitor). It took a while, but the results were that his heart was fine. The entire episode was caused by stress. The upcoming review board, his finances, and the uncertainty about his future, seem to have caused his heart to beat wildly, his face to flush, and all the other symptoms.

Jerry said he couldn't believe it when the doctor told him that the incident was caused by stress. He said, ''When I stopped worrying about everything, it all stopped.''

Wellness Affirmation

STRESS: I can control my stress. Stress is good until it gets out of hand. I rarely let stress get the best of me. I have time to relax and enjoy life. I set my priorities and remember not to worry about the things I cannot change.

LIFESTYLE AND LIFE EXPECTANCY

Everything in this book on wellness relates to how to improve the length and quality of your life. Life expectancy is the number of years a person will most likely live. Rates differ depending on diet, where people live, their occupation, and their genetics.

SOME INFORMATION ON LIFE EXPECTANCY

The current average life expectancy at birth of a person in the U.S. is approximately 75 years. Blacks tend to die earlier than whites (blacks 69.4 years, whites 75.6 years), largely due to infant mortality, AIDs, homicide, and poor medical care.

Even the car you drive may affect how long you will live. The Insurance Institute for Highway Safety measures the number of driver and passenger deaths for different vehicles registered in the United States. Each year they publish the results.

"AMAZING BUCK HELM...AN EARTHQUAKE MIRACLE"

In spite of our efforts, nature often has the final say concerning our health, our safety, and our future. You have control over most aspects of your wellness. However, medical background and history cannot be overlooked as you start healthy habits. An existing medical condition wrote a sad final chapter to what was one of the miracle stories of the 80s.

Buck Helm survived the 1989 California earthquake after being trapped for 89 hours in his car under a collapsed section of the I-880 Freeway. What the Great Quake of 89 couldn't do, a pre-existing medical condition could.

That earthquake dealt a heavy blow to Buck, but that's not what killed him 5 weeks later. He survived bruised lungs, three rib fractures, a skull fracture, and even kidney failure. He had come off the kidney dialysis machine and was about to be taken off the respirator when he took a turn for the worse.

Helm already suffered from hypertension, diabetes, and high blood pressure. The final blow was primarily due to undetected severe artery disease. Even before the big quake, Buck Helm had an enlarged heart and extensive blockage of the arteries supplying blood to his heart muscle. Unfortunately, doctors said it would have been only a matter of time before his general health did what the earthquake could not do to Buck Helm.

WHAT AFFECTS LIFE EXPECTANCY?

The list below contains some of the factors that determine how long you will live. You'll notice that there are more items on the list you can control than ones where you have little or no influence. Check which ones you can control.

Can Control	Cannot Control	
☐	☐	1. Who your parents and grandparents were partially determines your life span.
☐	☐	2. Your occupation correlates with length of life.
☐	☐	3. Seat belt use saves lives.
☐	☐	4. High blood pressure shortens life.
☐	☐	5. Whether or not you smoke affects your life expectancy.
☐	☐	6. Accidents are a major killer (especially among young people).
☐	☐	7. A high level of stress worsens disease and illness.
☐	☐	8. Early medical diagnosis helps, the sooner the better.
☐	☐	9. Where you live and your lifestyle make a difference.
☐	☐	10. Whether or not you are married is a factor. Married people live longer.
☐	☐	11. Your diet cleans you out or clogs you up.
☐	☐	12. Daily activity is better than being sedentary.

WHAT WILL YOU DO TO LIVE LONGER?

Use the space below to write down which items listed above could use some more attention in your life. (You can't change your parents.) Add anything you plan to do that's not on the list.

_____

_____

_____

_____

_____

_____

MONICA WANTS TO LIVE FOREVER!

Monica's lifestyle was so rushed that she never used a seat belt. She hadn't seen her doctor in three years, and smoked to calm her nerves. She read the list on page 68 and decided to make some lifestyle changes. She wrote a scene from her life as she'd like it to be six months from now.

Monica saw herself picking up the phone making a doctor's appointment for a physical. Someone was smoking nearby and the smell made her uncomfortable. She saw herself hanging up the phone and walking to her car without lighting up a cigarette. She saw herself fastening her seatbelt before starting the car. Next, she arrived early for her lunch date, and parked five blocks away to get a little walking in before and after lunch. At lunch she ordered a turkey sandwich on wheat bread, iced tea, and a small salad with oil and vinegar dressing.

Can you tell that Monica has mentally started a new lifestyle? Put yourself in her place and see if you can make those good changes really happen in your life. It takes some thinking and some planning, but it's definitely worth it.

Write the lifestyle you would like six months from now in the space below:

_____

_____

_____

_____

_____

_____

_____

_____

_____

_____

PART III

HELPING OTHERS WITH WELLNESS

HELPING OTHERS WITH WELLNESS

As your health improves, you will probably want others to get the same benefits. When we feel healthy, we want parents, children, spouses, lovers, and close friends to take better care of themselves. There's nothing wrong with this. But we may forget how hard it was for us to change or how many years we've been working on wellness activities.

Positive reinforcement is one of the most powerful ways to change others. This involves quickly rewarding a behavior with something positive, fun, or exciting. Our brain remembers the positive association between what we did and the nice things that happened afterward. The tendency is to do it again.

Punishment can also change behavior—for a short time. But it's the least effective way of getting someone to do something on their own for very long. Punishment occurs when a behavior is followed by something unpleasant or painful. There are often predictable emotional side effects when punishment is used.

SOUNDS TERRIBLE...TOO MUCH CONTROL

Maybe you shouldn't try to change people? However, you are probably already very instrumental in changing other people.

Where do you already influence others?

☐ staff meetings   ☐ meal times   ☐ school
☐ vacations   ☐ interviews   ☐ church
☐ training classes   ☐ gym class   ☐ performance evaluations
☐ traffic   ☐ Other _____   ☐ Other _____

CAN YOU CHANGE?

CAN YOU CHANGE?

Can you make these eleven changes for 72 hours? If you can master these changes—you might be able to change someone else's behavior. But chances are you will find these changes difficult. Try to see if you can:

1. Brush your teeth or hair in the other direction.

2. Eat with the other hand.

3. Wash with the other hand, switch to a sponge, a cloth, or just soap.

4. Tie knots backwards for shoelaces, etc.

5. Wear garments with colors, shapes, or styles that you don't usually wear.

6. Avoid watching television, even for news, sports, or comedy shows.

7. Wear your watch, ring, or bracelet on the other wrist or hand.

8. Switch to a radio station you never would listen to.

9. Sleep at different times than normal.

10. Sleep without a pillow (or with one, if you usually sleep without one).

11. Switch your favorite drink to one you usually avoid.

Habits are difficult to change because of inertia. Inertia is the "resistance to motion, action, or change." The eleven items above show how much inertia you have in each area. A person's habits only change when the motivation to change is stronger than the inertia.

The next few pages will present ideas on helping other people make positive changes to improve their wellness. The six areas covered are:

1. **WELLNESS REASON**—Clear reasons to change their lifestyle.
2. **MOTIVATION**—How badly do they want or need to change?
3. **HISTORY**—What successes and failures have they already had?
4. **ENABLERS**—Who or what allows them to continue in their present lifestyle pattern?
5. **NATURAL BENEFITS**—Positive consequences they can expect from improved wellness.
6. **IMPOSED CONSEQUENCES**—Your influence that will help them make the changes.

HELPING OTHER ADULTS WITH WELLNESS

> *"Only a life lived for others is a life worth while."* —*Albert Einstein*

1. **WELLNESS REASON:** Consider whether the person needs to make some changes due to current minor health problems or trends. These might include excess weight, fatigue, poor mental attitude, or simply a sedentary lifestyle. Be sure that major health issues get the attention of a qualified medical professional.

2. **MOTIVATION:** Think about how badly this adult wants to make changes in his or her life. If the person's motivation is very low, your personal example of a healthy lifestyle may be the best motivator. But remember, everyone chooses their way of living. Many who don't necessarily mimic our personal lifestyle still lead healthy and happy lives.

3. **HISTORY:** If they've tried before and failed it will be more difficult to get them to launch into a new effort. You'll need to hit it from a fresh angle.

4. **ENABLERS:** What allows them to continue in their present lifestyle?

☐ spouse   ☐ kids   ☐ denial
☐ job   ☐ parents   ☐ physical limitation
☐ Other _____   ☐ Other _____   ☐ Other _____

5. **NATURAL BENEFITS:** What are the positive consequences they will see as they begin to change?

☐ weight loss   ☐ clothes size   ☐ facial appearance
☐ respiration   ☐ better mental outlook ☐ strength
☐ flexibility   ☐ less coughing   ☐ Other _____
☐ Other _____   ☐ Other _____   ☐ Other _____

6. **IMPOSED CONSEQUENCES:** These are the things you can influence. What are the areas where you have positive influence in their lives? Where can you (1) use positive rewards and (2) remove negatives in their lives?

☐ social visits   ☐ hobbies   ☐ recreation
☐ romance   ☐ photographs   ☐ participate with them
☐ small purchases   ☐ meals   ☐ introductions
☐ praise   ☐ Other _____   ☐ Other _____

HELPING CHILDREN WITH WELLNESS

1. **WELLNESS REASON:** Kids build habits each day of their young lives. The eating, exercising, and relaxation habits they develop during the early years have a good chance of helping them in the future. Be sure that major health issues get the attention of a qualified medical professional.

2. **MOTIVATION:** Kids are motivated by fun and exciting things. They especially enjoy these activities in the presence of adults who add security and direction to their lives. Anything forced or prolonged can easily turn around and become demotivating to kids and teenagers. Teens will usually want more independence—but early habits, sports, and hobbies will often resurface later.

3. **HISTORY:** If a child has been frightened, pushed too hard, or injured while doing something healthy, they may have already formed a negative opinion. The path would be to try something new and connect it to what they already enjoy or look forward to.

4. **ENABLERS:** Who or what allows the child to remain unhealthy?

☐ mother ☐ stepparent ☐ school friend(s)
☐ other relative ☐ father ☐ school teacher
☐ babysitter ☐ hectic lifestyle ☐ Other _____
☐ Other _____ ☐ Other _____ ☐ Other _____

5. **NATURAL BENEFITS:** What will naturally happen as the child becomes more healthy?

☐ lose weight ☐ better at sports ☐ more friends
☐ get on sports team ☐ better in school ☐ girlfriend/boyfriend
☐ Other _____ ☐ Other _____ ☐ Other _____

6. **IMPOSED CONSEQUENCES:** What positive things can you do to make the child want to become more healthy?

☐ allowance ☐ television ☐ vacation
☐ stories ☐ parties ☐ movies
☐ your time and attention ☐ social time ☐ Other _____
☐ Other _____ ☐ Other _____ ☐ Other _____

HELPING SENIORS WITH WELLNESS

> *"Anyone who stops learning is old, whether at twenty or eighty. Anyone who keeps learning stays young. The greatest thing in life is to keep your mind young."*
> —Henry Ford

1. **WELLNESS REASON:** Many age-related problems used to be thought of as a normal part of getting old. The thinking is now changing. Evidence shows that a sedentary and inactive lifestyle causes physical and mental deterioration. Seniors can make significant improvements in their wellness by staying active. Be sure that major health issues get the attention of a qualified medical professional.

2. **MOTIVATION:** Like anyone else, seniors have various levels of motivation. Some will jump at the chance to become more active and healthy. Others will prefer to continue with the routine they've become accustomed to. As usual, no one should be forced to do something they prefer not to do.

3. **HISTORY:** Take some time to learn about their past history. They may have engaged in activities you've never discussed. Not only will it spark their interest, you might hear some great stories. Use this as a stepping stone to get them introduced to new activities or reintroduced to the ones they used to love.

4. **ENABLERS:** What allows them to continue in the unhealthy situation they're in?

   ☐ adult children   ☐ grand children   ☐ spouse
   ☐ care provider   ☐ social group (organized)
   ☐ social friends   ☐ physician   ☐ medication
   ☐ Other _____   ☐ Other _____   ☐ Other _____

5. **NATURAL BENEFITS:** Consider some of the short term benefits that would interest the senior.

   ☐ youthful appearance ☐ live longer   ☐ more active
   ☐ increased mobility ☐ less pain   ☐ fewer injuries
   ☐ faster recovery ☐ romance   ☐ Other _____
   ☐ Other _____   ☐ Other _____   ☐ Other _____

6. **IMPOSED CONSEQUENCES:** Where do you fit in? Are there some positives you can influence them with?

   ☐ personal visits   ☐ family visits   ☐ gifts
   ☐ participate with them ☐ include them in outings
   ☐ letters   ☐ phone calls   ☐ travel
   ☐ Other _____   ☐ Other _____   ☐ Other _____

FAMILY WELLNESS

It is hard to watch your health and take responsibility for your personal wellness when those you live with don't. Your living situation will have profound effects on two areas of your wellness. These are: Your current level of health and your future maintenance of today's wellness gains.

WHAT YOU CAN DO WITH YOUR SPOUSE OR SIGNIFICANT OTHER

1. *Cross Boundaries.* Ask your partner what he or she likes to do for sports or general activities. Plan to spend time learning and doing this activity. In time both of you can learn to enjoy healthy activities together.

2. *Weekly Suspense.* Try the fishbowl idea. Put several pieces of paper in a medium-size bowl or box. On each piece of paper list an activity. For instance, one couple listed the following items on the pieces of paper:

- movie
- dancing
- restaurant
- shopping
- skating
- bowling

On the nights you decide to become active, pick a piece of paper and do what is written on it.

3. *Brand-new Area.* Learn a new skill or hobby together. Pick something that neither you or your partner has had any experience in. For example, you might decide to:

- Take a Japanese cooking class
- Learn to scuba dive
- Visit a museum
- Take a cooking course
- Take up mountain biking

JOE IS NOT FEELING WELL

Joe is unhappy with his life. He's too busy at work to produce the high-quality technical drawings he used to. Joe skips lunch every day and downs 6–10 cups of coffee by two in the afternoon. His wife and kids haven't complained, but he knows something is wrong. Their time together isn't what it used to be. Joe is exhausted by Wednesday and actually feels ill by Friday.

His wife says he should either get a checkup or stop turning down invitations from their friends. Joe's boss remarked that it's normal for work quality to slip once in a while, but Joe's poor attitude causes him concern. The boss offered Joe a few days off so he could pull things together. Joe snapped back that he didn't need special treatment. That was Monday. Joe went home at noon that day feeling lousy. He wondered if Tuesday would be better. Maybe he could catch up on sleep this weekend.

Does Joe need to change?

HELP YOUR CHILDREN STAY WELL

Here are some suggestions for your children's wellness.

Television: Limit television viewing. Try to encourage educational programs or shows where the entire family an watch as a group.

Competition: Build in plenty of low to moderate competition. Keep it friendly and relaxed. When appropriate, include a small amount of moderate to heavy competition. For some children this can cement the need for wellness, if they learn to see it as a tool for better performance.

Stories: Reading aloud to children has long been associated with improved results in school. How about adding a bit on wellness? The heroes of action-packed stories need healthy bodies and clear minds. Pause from time to time to emphasize these two areas.

Record Keeping: You may wish to monitor each child's progress in meeting and surpassing these goals. Early habits tend to last.

Testing Kids for Fitness: In the United States, since 1943, kids have been tested for levels of fitness at some point in school. The test has evolved quite a bit. Today it focuses on four specific areas:
1. Endurance run
2. Pull-ups (boys) or flexed arm-hang (girls)
3. Sit and reach
4. Sit ups

Passing levels have declined during the past 10 years, from 43 percent in the early 1980s to 32 percent entering the 1990s.

WE MISSED!
Americans Failed Fitness Goals, Say Centers for Disease Control

Although more companies offer fitness programs and more doctors are asking about exercise history when they examine new patients, many of the nation's fitness goals will be missed as we enter the 1990s.

The government's ten-year ''Objectives for the Nation'' that are being missed are:
- Getting 60 percent of adults to do 20 minutes of vigorous exercise three times a week.
- Having 60 percent of 10–17-year-olds participate in daily physical education programs in school.
- Getting 50 percent of elderly Americans to exercise three times a week.
- Having more than 90 percent of children aged 10–17 participate in three weekly vigorous exercise sessions.

FAMILY WELLNESS CHART

You're getting used to this by now. Your family 28-day chart is a tool to make your progress visible and rewarding. When it becomes a chore, or a source of guilt, toss it. By that time it has lost its usefulness.

This chart measures minutes of activity with a family member. Passive activities like television and videos don't count. Start either today or tomorrow. Begin with an easy, achievable goal, and to be consistent, fill out the chart at the same time each day.

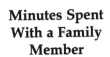

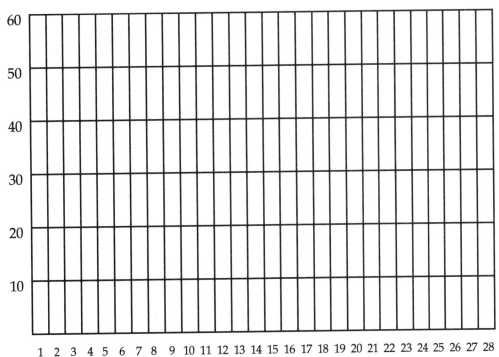

28-Day Family Chart

Days of Successful Family Activities

"IF YOU CAN DO IT FOR 28 DAYS...YOU CAN DO IT FOREVER"

THE MISSING DAYS ARE GETTING CLOSE!

PART IV

SEXUALLY TRANSMITTED DISEASES AND CANCER

SEXUALLY TRANSMITTED DISEASES

> *"Sex is a biological fact which is hard to evaluate psychologically."*
> —Sigmund Freud

Sexually Transmitted Diseases, or STDs, are diseases that are passed from one person to another by intimate physical contact. They are also referred to as venereal diseases (VD).

- Some STDs do not have noticeable symptoms.
- There are over 20 different STDs.
- The risk of contracting an STD increases with the number of sexual partners.
- You can spread an STD without knowing it.
- A few STDs are as prevalent as the common cold.
- In the United States, someone is infected with an STD every 12 seconds.

Some of the more common sexual diseases are syphilis, gonorrhea, and herpes. Following is a brief description of these three. A more in-depth treatment of AIDS follows.

1. **Syphilis.** Syphilis is caused by a microorganism. It progresses through four distinct stages. Stage 1 occurs 2–5 weeks after exposure to the organism. Often there are chancre sores that look like pimples or blisters. They are often painless and go unnoticed. Stage 2 occurs 3–6 weeks later. It is accompanied by a mild skin rash; flu-like symptoms such as stomach ache and headache; and sores, eye inflammation, and even falling hair. Stage 3 is the latent stage, where it appears the person is cured. Stage 4 is called the late stage. In this stage, serious damage is done to the nervous system, heart and eyes. About 30 percent of cases do not progress past Stage 1, but an unfortunate 30 percent go all the way to the late stage long after the sufferer thought the disease had disappeared.

2. **Gonorrhea.** This disease has reached epidemic proportions. Some believe it is as prevalent as the common cold. It is a bacterial disease with symptoms 3–10 days after exposure. Men will experience a penile discharge and pain while urinating. Many women do not notice any symptoms. In men, gonorrhea can lead to sperm duct damage. In women it often leads to pelvic inflammatory disease (PID). Women and men suffer from infertility when the disease is not detected or treated properly. Gonorrhea is one of the STDs that adapts itself to medications, requiring heavier doses of different treatments. There are five places where gonorrhea strikes: (1) the cervix in women, (2) the urethra in men, (3) the anus, (4) the throat, and (5) the eyes. It's unfortunate that the symptoms in women often go unnoticed—the estimate of undetected cervical gonorrhea in women is 80 percent. This lack of detection is blamed for much of the spread of the disease.

SEXUALLY TRANSMITTED DISEASES (Continued)

3. **Herpes.** Herpes Simplex Virus I strikes primarily above the waist and Herpes Simples Virus II typically occurs in the genital area. Herpes II is implicated in cervical cancer in women. It involves a primary attack about 1 week following direct contact with an infected person. It disappears after 2–3 weeks, but, unfortunately is followed by lifetime outbreaks of the contagious sores and secretions. These recurrences are milder than the initial attack and nowadays are becoming much more manageable. The person is still highly contagious during these outbreaks. U.S. statistics show that 17 percent of the population is infected with the genital herpes virus. Detailed figures show infection rates of 14 percent of those who never married, 16 percent of married people, and 35 percent of divorced people. Sixty percent of those who have genital herpes may never know they have it.

4. **AIDS.** Acquired Immune Deficiency Syndrome (AIDS) has received worldwide attention because of its epidemic spread and near-certainty of death once it is contracted. A rough breakdown shows that in the U.S. over 60 percent of AIDS cases involve homosexual or bisexual men. About 20 percent of the cases are intravenous drug users. About 4–6 percent of the cases involve heterosexual men and women. Many of the remaining cases are from blood transfusions and childbirth.

The AIDS virus is not hearty and cannot live very long when exposed to air, soap, chlorine, or heat. This suggests some very predictable ways it must be passed along from one infected person to another. At the same time, it gives us some security to develop precautionary procedures to slow the spread of the disease.

AIDS is a complex issue involving disease, fear, privacy, research, and death. Like many diseases from the past, the confusion surrounding AIDS clouds the issue and points blame at groups and individuals.

MORE ON AIDS

EXPOSURE. Exchange of body fluid with an infected person, or contact with a contaminated body fluid.

HIV. (Human Immunodeficiency Virus). The scientific term for the AIDS virus.

ARC. (Aids-Related Complex). This is the stage of general ailments such as swollen lymph glands, diarrhea, fatigue, or night sweats. At this point, the person does not have one of the specific diseases under the heading of AIDS.

AIDS. (Acquired Immune Deficiency Syndrome). The diagnosis is confirmed when the person's immune system deteriorates and allows a specific infection or tumor to occur. The presence of one of the opportunistic infections, such as Karposi's sarcoma (skin cancer), or lymphoma (malignancy of the lymph glands) establishes the formal medical diagnosis of AIDS. The victim dies as a result of one of these infections and not from the HIV virus.

AIDS (Continued)

The facts clearly show that the AIDS virus is passed from one person to another in some very specific ways. Although new information continually adds to our knowledge, many things we feared would spread the virus such as mosquito bites have not been proven to be a risk. At most, there is a miniscule possibility of acquiring AIDS other than the high risk behaviors explained below.

Families with children were initially afraid that an HIV-positive child might pass the virus along to other children. Although kids share food, popsicles, kisses, and toys, none of these has been responsible for passing the virus. AIDS is difficult (if not impossible) to pass along casually.

If AIDS can't be passed along casually, how do you get the disease? Listed below are the ways AIDS is transmitted and a list of high-risk activities.

AIDS is contracted by the exchange of bodily fluids with an infected person. An infected person is someone who has antibodies in the blood that are attempting to fight the virus. There are tests which tell whether the antibodies are present or not.

HOW AIDS IS TRANSMITTED

1. Sexual contact: vaginal or anal intercourse.
2. Blood transfusions.
3. Intravenous drug use.
4. Childbirth: the baby can be infected from the mother before, during, or shortly after delivery.

HIGH-RISK ACTIVITIES

- Intercourse with prostitutes
- Sex with several partners
- Anal intercourse
- Sharing hypodermic needles
- Sex with a sexually promiscuous partner

AIDS PROGRESS

There are signs that the medical community's efforts, combined with lifestyle changes among the population, are making progress in fighting the AIDS epidemic.

DRUG THERAPY

New drugs on the market show promise in the fight against AIDS. Up to now the progression from exposure through the various stages has been predictable and swift. New therapy including the drug AZT (zidovudine) tends to slow the progress of the disease. This is starting to dispel the perception that once a person has AIDS their life is over. People diagnosed with AIDS are remaining at work longer and staying healthy for more extended periods of time.

SLOWER EPIDEMIC

Although still controversial, many researchers and investigators are suggesting that the rate of the epidemic is slowing. Great Britain has seen a peak in the number of reported infections. Positive signs have also come from the gay community. Gays were hit very hard during the beginning of the epidemic. Some reports show the disease beginning to level off among homosexuals. A few cities show a slower rate of infection.

BETTER AWARENESS

Gays, adults in their 30s and above, and the medical profession have made the best lifestyle and procedural changes to halt the spread of the disease. These groups have learned the specific ways AIDS is spread and have successfully taken steps to publicize this information. More people are learning that the disease is preventable and the virus is weak. Intravenous drug users continue to have a very high infection rate.

VACCINE

When Edward Jenner developed the smallpox vaccine, he went on a hunch that dairy workers who had contracted cowpox were somehow protected from the deadly smallpox. Today, researchers are hopeful that recent success in vaccinating monkeys against AIDS will eventually have positive applications for humans. But they warn that progress is slow and there are major barriers to coming up with a vaccine for humans.

AVOIDING SEXUALLY TRANSMITTED DISEASES

There are several precautions you can take to reduce the chance of being exposed to, contracting, and spreading a sexually transmitted disease. These involve a combination of open communication with intimate partners and specific activities that make sexual contact safer. Look at the list below, and check the precautions you are already taking. Then check the precautions you intend to start taking.

AVOIDING DISEASE	I'm doing this now.	I intend to start doing this today.
1. Discuss sexually transmitted diseases with your partner.	☐	☐
2. Limit the number of sex partners.	☐	☐
3. Use barrier contraceptives, especially condoms.	☐	☐
4. Wash with warm soap and water before and after intercourse.	☐	☐
5. Urinate after intercourse (men).	☐	☐
6. Schedule annual Pap smears for early detection of cervical cancer (women).	☐	☐

Let's show that Freud was wrong when he summed up human sexual responsibility in these words: ''Do you not know how uncontrolled and unreliable the average human being is in all that concerns sex?''

Education, precautions, and safe sex are even more significant when discussing the most deadly STD to come along in recent history. The following discussion of AIDS will go into more detail than the other sexual diseases you just read about.

Wellness Affirmation

STD's including AIDS: STD's are preventable. I take reasonable precautions, without becoming fanatical or unreasonably paranoid. I can be instrumental in reducing the suffering caused by this disease.

CANCER

Cancer is another major killer. Many people are frightened by cancer and tend to avoid discussing it or learning about the disease. The good news is that most of the time, cancer can be cured and there are several things a person can do to beat or treat the disease.

CANCER WARNING SIGNS

1. Change in a wart or mole (size, color, shape)
2. Unusual bleeding or discharge
3. Sores that don't heal
4. Unexplained loss of weight or appetite
5. A lump or thickening
6. Unusual hoarseness, nagging cough
7. Change in bowel or bladder habits

LIFESTYLE HABITS FOR LOW CANCER RISK

- Low intake of red meat
- Physically active lifestyle
- Low intake of processed foods
- Little or no smoking or tobacco use
- Moderate or no alcohol consumption
- Regular medical checkups (for early diagnosis)

EARLY DETECTION IS IMPORTANT

Early detection saves lives. Learn the proper method to locate lumps, enlargement, or changes in consistency. Take 2–3 minutes each month to perform self examinations in these areas:

- breasts
- testicles
- skin
- mouth

Make appointments with your doctor to check for cancer of the: (1) breast, (2) uterus, (3) colon and rectum, (4) prostate.

LIFESTYLE CHANGES AND CANCER

Many people think of cancer as a mystery disease that strikes when and where it chooses. They feel there is little they can do to avoid it or recover from it once it strikes. Contrary to this thinking, the disease is becoming less mysterious, and there is plenty you can do to fight it.

The way we live has a lot to do with whether or not we get cancer. It is not contagious, or inherited. It cannot be caused by blows or injuries. It is however, connected to certain activities and lifestyles. Consider the following:

- Japanese women get just 15–20% of their calories from fat (a very low percentage). Their incidence of **breast cancer** is far below that of women in the Unites States.

- **Colon cancer** is a Western ailment. Cancer of this portion of the large intestine seems to be connected with low fiber intake. In cultures where dietary fiber intake is high, colon cancer is almost non-existent.

- Those exposed to sun can reduce their incidence of cataracts and **skin cancer** by wearing sunglasses and hats.

It is possible to protect yourself against many forms of cancer through your lifestyle.

AVOIDING CANCER

You can considerably lower your chances of getting cancer, or surviving cancer by following some basic guidelines and watching for the 7 warning signs listed on page 88.

Some of the guidelines that will help you reduce your cancer risk are:
1. Follow the Anti-Cancer Diet
    A. Eat high fiber foods.
    B. Eat foods high in Vitamin C.
    C. Eat a wide variety of vegetables.
    D. Lower fat and cholesterol intake.
    E. Bake, broil, stir-fry and steam foods rather than sauteeing and deep fat frying.
2. Stop smoking/Don't start
3. Guard skin from too much sunlight
4. Drink alcohol in moderation

What I Can Do To Follow The 4 Guidelines

A. _____
B. _____
C. _____
D. _____

AVOIDING CANCER

THINGS TO AVOID:

UNMANAGED STRESS—

Type of cancer: Prolonged stress weakens the immune system making your body less resistant to invading cancer cells.

How to reduce risk: Practice stress reduction and coping skills on a daily basis. Include moderate exercise and leisure activities into your lifestyle.

POOR DIET—

Type of cancer: Colon, rectum, stomach, and uterine can be the end result of a consistently poor diet.

How to reduce risk: Eat low fat and cholesterol foods. Add fresh fruit and vegetables to your diet.

SMOKING—

Type of cancer: Smoking may contribute to lung, mouth, larynx, uterus, kidney, esophagus, bladder, pancreas and stomach cancer.

How to reduce risk: Stop smoking cigarettes.

SUN EXPOSURE—

Type of cancer: Excessive sun exposure is associated with skin cancer. Watch for lumps or moles that grow, ooze, bleed, or change in any way.

How to reduce risk: Avoid peak sun hours (11 am to 2 pm). Use appropriate coverings, hats or umbrellas along with a sunscreen (SPF 15 or greater).

HEAVY DRINKING—

Type of cancer: Excessive drinking is linked to cancer of the mouth, jaw, cheek, throat, esophagus, tonsils, liver, and pancreas.

How to reduce risk: Don't drink more than 1–2 drinks per day. Drinking combined with smoking heightens the risk of cancer.

WORKPLACE HAZARDS—

Type of cancer: Contact with certain chemicals can lead to various types of cancers. Watch for the 7 warning signs.

How to reduce risk: Wear protective clothing to avoid contact with chemicals, dusts, metals, and fibers. Wear safety equipment and follow safety procedures.

ESTROGEN/DRUGS—

Type of cancer: Estrogen and DES (Diethyl Stilbesterol) are often linked to uterine cancer. Prescription drugs are, at times, linked to other types of cancers.

How to reduce risk: Check with your doctor so that you thoroughly understand the risks and benefits of drug therapy. Don't be intimidated or fearful that you are taking too much of the doctor's time or asking too many questions.

OBESITY—

Type of cancer: Related to colon, uterine, prostate, and breast cancer.

How to reduce risk: Learn about and maintain proper weight for your age and body type. Eat the right foods and exercise regularly, moderately and consistently.

So you see, there really is a lot you can do to control your risk of cancer. Take another look at each of the areas and see where you, your family and even some of your friends may need to make some improvement.

My Improvement Plan

UNMANAGED STRESS:

Personal changes _____

Family changes _____

Work changes _____

POOR DIET:

Personal changes _____

Family changes _____

Work changes _____

SMOKING:

Personal changes _____

Family changes _____

Work changes _____

My Improvement Plan (continued)

SUN EXPOSURE:

    Personal changes _____

    Family changes _____

    Work changes _____

HEAVY DRINKING:

    Personal changes _____

    Family changes _____

    Work changes _____

WORKPLACE HAZARDS:

    Personal changes _____

    Family changes _____

    Work changes _____

ESTROGEN/DRUGS:

    Personal changes _____

    Family changes _____

    Work changes _____

OBESITY:

    Personal changes _____

    Family changes _____

    Work changes _____

PART V

ACHIEVING BALANCE

BALANCING YOUR LIFE

> *"There is no more fatal blunderer than he who consumes the greater part of his life getting his living."*
> —*Henry David Thoreau*

HOW BALANCED PEOPLE LIVE...WHAT THEY BELIEVE

Balanced people tend to sit back, take a deep breath and evaluate the way they work and live. They believe that doing too many things is what gets people out of balance. They have learned to say no to things that would get their lives out of balance. Following are some examples of commitments that set balance. Put a check mark next to those that are a part of your life. Then check those that you intend to add to your life. Add more activities to the list if you can.

BALANCE YOUR LIFE	I'm doing this already.	I intend to start doing this today.
1. A regular date at the gym with friends	☐	☐
2. 2–3 lunch appointments a week	☐	☐
3. Vacation paid for in advance	☐	☐
4. A standing movie night with rotating carpool drivers	☐	☐
5. Annual sign-ups for team sports (they depend on you to show up)	☐	☐
6. Membership on select committees at church, social clubs, or in the community	☐	☐

7. Other commitments: _____

_____

_____

These items and many more are part of the balanced person's life. Without thinking about it, their system of commitments leads them to balance.

BALANCE DISORDERS

Lifestyle balance problems include excessive time pressures, personal life deterioration, and family compromises. These problems can be improved by priority management, balanced values, and well-rounded activities. Some of the causes of lifestyle balance problems are:

- Unrealistic expectations
- Confused goals and priorities
- Poor interpersonal skills
- Job insecurity

UNDERSTANDING BALANCE

> **Balance is:** A stable, calm state of the emotions . . . A satisfying arrangement marked by even distribution of elements . . . Characterized by the display of symmetry.

Priority management, balanced values, and well-rounded activities fall into two broad balance categories: **macro,** or universal balance; and **micro,** or local balance.

1. MACRO BALANCE (Universal)

The large, universal picture of your life includes the major segments you feel are most important. You might call these your core values. These values constitute the important pieces of your life that need to be symmetrical—that need to be in macro balance. In the diagram below, circle your core values (add any that aren't listed already).

HEALTH

SPIRITUAL   HOBBIES

SOCIAL   EDUCATION

SPOUSE   YOUR
                              LIFE   WORK

KIDS   NUTRITION

EXERCISE   _____

_____

When one area becomes troubled, you need to have an evenly distributed lifestyle that carries you through.

2. MICRO BALANCE (Local)

You've scrutinized all the important segments of your life to check for **macro balance.** This big picture can also be looked at under a microscope to see that each separate segment is internally balanced. This is what we call **micro** balance. Look at the diagrams below. In each cluster, circle the values that you feel are important. Add any values that aren't listed already.

personal contribution

team contribution

_____

```
┌──────────────┐
│    YOUR      │
│    WORK      │
└──────────────┘
```

routine paperwork

challenge/adventure

growth

group worship

private meditation

_____

```
┌──────────────┐
│    YOUR      │
│ SPIRITUAL LIFE│
└──────────────┘
```

_____

family values

strength

flexibility

_____

```
┌──────────────┐
│    YOUR      │
│   EXERCISE   │
└──────────────┘
```

_____

cardiovascular

classes

related reading

_____

```
┌──────────────────────┐
│   YOUR EDUCATION      │
│   AND GROWTH          │
└──────────────────────┘
```

_____

extra reading

When you combine macro and micro balance, you add to your personal wellness in tangible ways. You become healthier, more relaxed, and even more effective at work and at home.

Look at the case about Maria and Paul on the next page. What do you think of the different types of equilibrium in their lives? What do you think their state of wellness will be in the future?

OUT OF BALANCE

> *"Destructiveness is the outcome of an unlived life."* —Erich Fromm

Maria and Paul are out of balance. During the first two years of their marriage they vowed to take good care of each other and stay well-rounded. They chose five important life areas to watch carefully: work, home, church, finances, and socializing.

Paul thought hobbies should be included, but Maria convinced him to keep the list to five. (Hobbies could be included in the "home" section.) The plan worked well until Maria got a promotion. Maria thought the new position was a chance to get her career moving. The extra pay from this and the next promotion would get them to their financial goals 3–5 years sooner. Paul noticed that the promotion initially revitalized Maria. She had extra energy that he could barely match. Unfortunately, it didn't last. The excitement and enthusiasm began to turn into anger and frustration. This didn't help their social calendar at all.

The few times Paul and Maria had free time, their friends always "had plans." Maria didn't care because with the next promotion she'd have access to "higher quality friends anyway." Paul got more and more confused and decided to take a short vacation—alone. Maybe things would settle down a bit if they had time to think about what went wrong.

What would you do to help Maria and Paul regain balance?

Wellness Affirmation

BALANCED LIFE: My life is balanced. I balance the major segments that are important for my future. When I go out of balance it's for short periods with a definite purpose. I also build balance inside of the major areas of my life. This gives me more energy, clearer thinking and better success.

HOW TO STAY BALANCED

How many of these suggestions do you follow already? How many do you think you'll start following? Check the boxes.

STAYING BALANCED	I'm doing this already.	I intend to start doing this today.
1. Hire outside help.	☐	☐
2. Identify your core values and turn them into priorities.	☐	☐
3. Develop and keep a positive attitude.	☐	☐
4. Improve your time-management and organizational skills.	☐	☐
5. Keep your expectations realistic.	☐	☐
6. Develop a support system.	☐	☐
7. Add personal and family items to your daily to-do list.	☐	☐
8. Delegate the right tasks to the right people.	☐	☐
9. Pick a standard weekday evening for a regular outing (dinner, bowling, a movie, etc.).	☐	☐
10. Write down goals you can achieve with some ''stretch.''	☐	☐
11. Love yourself—take time to show it.	☐	☐
12. Double your phone calls—keep them short but frequent.	☐	☐
13. Develop a system for reliable child care.	☐	☐
14. Select employers or employees who believe in balance.	☐	☐
15. Say NO to ideas and projects that will take you out of balance for too long.	☐	☐

''Only great minds can afford a simple style.''	—Stendhal

HOW TO STAY BALANCED (Continued)

PETS AND HEALTHY PEOPLE

" AN APPLE A DAY IS OK ... BUT A COCKER SPANIEL MAY BE BETTER"

You may be accused of having a zoo in the living room, but pets have a definite way of balancing out your life and reducing stress at the same time. If your life doesn't include dogs, cats, birds, or even fish, you may be missing a neat way to stay healthy. Before picking the critter and hauling it home, though, take some time to read up on the type you've selected. This will save time and headaches (and carpet) for you, and lots of pain and suffering for the pet.

DOGS.   This "best friend" can be ideal for health and balance if you don't mind the care and attention many dogs require. Leaving town creates special challenges, but the friendship, companionship, and love easily make up for it.

CATS.   Felines can be finicky and aloof. If you're prepared for cuddling on their terms, a cat can be a pleasant addition to your lifestyle. Because of their independence they don't require as much care as a dog. Some owners feel that cats tend to need a bit more medical care.

BIRDS.   Parakeets and cockatiels make good starter pets. A good cage, a supply of feed, and regular care will do. Spend plenty of time touching and holding a young bird. This will make it a friendlier pet as it grows. Birds are quite sensitive to heat, cold, drafts, and cats! The only nuisance might be when you plan to sleep until ten and the bird starts singing at seven.

FISH.   A fish tank can be tricky. Start small and stick to goldfish and guppies. This will give you time to learn how to manage an aquarium and to see if the care required suits your temperament. If yes, you will find an amazing and relaxing world of underwater life.

TAKE A HIKE ... FOR BALANCE!

Want a new way to relax, get some exercise, and breathe good crisp air? Orienteering may be just for you. What's orienteering? Taking a map and a compass and then getting lost in the forest.

Actually, many complete the 4–5 kilometer course without losing track of direction. The idea is to follow a course through various checkpoints and make it to the end in as little time as possible. There are several levels of courses, requiring increasingly greater navigational skills.

Worried about taking up the whole day? Relax! The courses usually take 1–2 hours to complete. Persons with moderate to advanced skills complete the most difficult courses in 1½ hours ... Of course those who never return aren't counted in the statistics!!!

Orienteering was invented around 1930 in Scandinavia, originally as a running game.

Contact: U.S. Orienteering Federation, P.O. Box 1444, Forest Park, GA 30051

WHAT ABOUT THE MISSING DAYS?

Your 28-day charts are meant to build good habits. This also included the habit of being flexible, human, and sociable. The missing days are for fun times. The only requirement is to have a good time—without doing damage to your wellness or the wellness of others. Use the extra days each month to try something different and reward yourself for the success and discipline you've shown all month long. You deserve it!

LET'S PARTY: The missing days are found!

16 things to do on the missing days:

1. Sleep in, or take a nap.
2. Eat out.
3. Buy some ice cream (or low-fat frozen yogurt).
4. Watch old movies.
5. Waste some time on something fun.
6. Talk with someone, anyone you want.
7. Take a sauna, jacuzzi, or whirlpool.
8. Plan a weekend at a bed-and-breakfast inn.
9. Check into a European health spa.
10. Take a trip.
11. Go wine tasting in a limousine.
12. Go for a fun walk in a special place.
13. Add to your wardrobe.
14. Have dinner delivered and rent movies.
15. Share a bottle of champagne at home.
16. Take some time off and _____.

> *"Moderation in temper is always a virtue, but moderation in principle is always a vice."*
> —*Thomas Paine*

Personal Wellness

REVIEW

Well, now you have it. We've covered many areas revolving around health, wellness, and well-being. You have a good idea of some of the things to do (exercise, eat well, take care of your heart and back), along with areas to control (cholesterol, smoking, weight, alcohol, drugs and stress). Remember to be careful when you wish to assist others with wellness. How did you do on changing your life for 72 hours? Your family and friends must **want to change** before you can be of much help.

The sexual diseases section may have been a reminder of what you already knew, or a fresh presentation of information you need to know. Keep reading about the AIDS epidemic. New findings are being published daily. Don't forget that early diagnosis by a competent professional gives you a better chance with any of the STDs, AIDS, or cancer.

A balanced life is everyone's goal. How to attain it is often the problem. The section on macro and micro balance was meant to help you along the way. Even if you simply think about the equilibrium in your life from time to time, you'll be moving toward improving it.

Finally, the missing days and the great excuses can be fun, refreshing, and humorous. If you find yourself making too many excuses, you may need to have more fun during the missing days to re-energize you. Life should be enjoyable.

As you read each section, some parts may have caught your attention more than others. There are three possible reasons for this:

1. It was a familiar area where you're already committed to wellness.
2. It was brand-new, interesting information.
3. The area was one that needs improvement in your life.

Let's make a quick assessment of these three possibilities. Write down what comes to mind for each one:

WHERE I'M DOING WELL:

_____

_____

NEW INFORMATION:

_____

_____

WHERE I NEED TO DO BETTER:

_____

_____

You've shown excellent responsibility for your wellness by reading this book. It took time and effort, but you made it. Now it's time to reward or acknowledge yourself for all the good things you're already doing. And it's time to begin taking action on the parts that can use some improvement.

Be careful not to tackle too much at any one time. Remember that your mind and body do not like sudden or drastic changes. You may react to too much change by getting sick, angry, frustrated, and even depressed. Try taking one solid step at a time. Build good habits around your first step and then launch into the next.

Changing your life takes time. It also requires many repetitions. Recall how many attempts it took to learn to ride a bicycle, to ski, or to drive a car. Reread *Personal Wellness* and other material on the subject. Avoid material or commercial programs that push one product or program to an extreme.

The controls are in your hands. Use them wisely. You have more influence over your physical and mental wellness than you may think. Good luck!

SOME GREAT EXCUSES!

I've had friends who were masters at excuses. In fact, they were so good, by the time they were done I would begin making a stronger case for them to show that I understood. Just in case you're not as adept as some of my friends, when you absolutely must have an excuse for missing a part of your wellness plan . . . here you go!

1. I got **caught in traffic** and couldn't make it to the gym.
2. There was this **show on TV** that I couldn't miss . . . it was educational.
3. I was with some friends and they all smoke.
4. It's too **cold** outside.
5. I need to clean the house/apartment.
6. I'm just too **tired** after a hard day at work.
7. The kids just wear me out . . . there's no energy left for balance.
8. I walk a lot at work from office to office.
9. I don't cook at home . . . how can I eat right?
10. It's too **hot** outside.
11. My **dog is sick** . . . I need to stay at home.
12. My video cassette recorder is broken . . . I can't do my taped exercise program.
13. I don't have the **right clothes** . . . I'll look out of place.
14. You can't get healthy food at restaurants.
15. It's too **nice** outside.
16. My doctor says to take it easy . . . so I'd better not do **anything.**
17. I've got a bad . . . (pick one or two) back, knee, ankle, wrist, elbow, big toe, finger, ear, nose, eye, tongue, eyebrow, mustache, eyelash.
18. I **weigh too much** to excercise.
19. My wife won't go with me.
20. My husband makes fun of me when I work out.
21. I don't weigh enough to exercise.
22. I simply **don't have time** for this silly stuff.
23. I can't risk getting hurt . . . I have a family to support.
24. My aquarium needs cleaning . . . again!
25. There's **no proof** that diet and exercise help you live better.

"No excuses . . . keep going."   —*coach Ed Taylor*

MORE READING FOR WELLNESS

Kirsta, Alix, *The Book of Stress Survival: Identifying and Reducing Stress in Your Life* (New York: Simon & Schuster, 1986).

Potter, Beverly, *Preventing Job Burnout: Transforming Work Pressures into Productivity* (Los Altos, CA: Crisp Publications, 1987).

Davis, Martha; Robbins Eshelman, Elizabeth; and Mckay, Matthew, *The Relaxation and Stress Reduction Workbook* (Oakland CA: New Harbinger Publications, 1988).

Mason, L. John, *Stress Passages: Surviving Life's Transitions Gracefully* (Berkeley, CA: Celestial Arts, 1988).

Benson, M.D., Herber; and Klipper, Miriam; *The Relaxation Response* (New York: William Morrow, 1975).

Borysenko, Joan, *Minding the Body, Mending the Mind* (New York: Bantam Books, 1988).

Copper, M.D., Kenneth, *The Aerobics Program for Total Well-Being* (New York: M. Evans, 1982).

Sorensen, Jacki, *Aerobics Lifestyle Book* (New York: Poseidon Press, 1983).

Griggs, Rick, *Professional Balance* (Mountain View, CA: MANFIT Publications, 1989).

Cooper, Robert, *Health and Fitness Excellence: The Scientific Action Plan* (Boston, MA: Houghton Mifflin, 1984).

Rayman, Rebecca, *The Body in Brief: Essentials for Health Care* (El Paso, TX: Skidmore-Roth, 1989).

Readers Digest, *Eat Better, Live Better: A Commonsense Guide to Nutrition and Good Health* (New York: The Readers Digest Association, 1982).

Bayrd, Ned and Quilter, Chris, *Food for Champions: How to Eat to Win* (Boston, MA: Houghton-Mifflin, 1982).

MORE READING FOR
WELLNESS (Continued)

Bailey, Covert, *Fit or Fat: A New Way to Health and Fitness through Nutrition and Aerobic Exercise* (Boston MA: Houghton-Mifflin, 1978).

Cooper, M.D., Kenneth, *Aerobics* (New York: M. Evans and Company, 1968).

Whitaker, M.D., Julian M., *Reversing Heart Disease: A Vital Program to Prevent, Treat and Eliminate Cardiac Problems without Surgery* (New York: Warner Books, 1985).

The American Medical Association, *Home Medical Advisor* (New York: Random House, 1988).

Samuels, M.D., Mike and Samuels, Nancy, *The Well Adult: The Complete Guide to Protecting and Improving Your Health* (New York: Summit Books, 1988).

Lowen, Alexander, *Love, Sex, and Your Heart* (New York: Macmillan, 1988).

Sherman, Marlene, *Wellness In The Workplace* (Los Altos, CA: Crisp Publications, 1990).

Dvorak, Robert, *Wellness At The Workstation* (Los Altos, CA: Crisp Publications, 1990).

NOTES

NOTES

NOTES

NOTES

NOTES

NOTES

NOTES

NOTES

OVER 150 BOOKS AND 35 VIDEOS AVAILABLE IN THE 50-MINUTE SERIES

50-Minute Series Books and Videos Subject Areas . . .

Management
Training
Human Resources
Customer Service and Sales Training
Communications
Small Business and Financial Planning
Creativity
Personal Development
Wellness
Adult Literacy and Learning
Career, Retirement and Life Planning

Other titles available from Crisp Publications in these categories

Crisp Computer Series
The Crisp Small Business & Entrepreneurship Series
Quick Read Series
Management
Personal Development
Retirement Planning